50 Things
You Didn't Know
About 1916

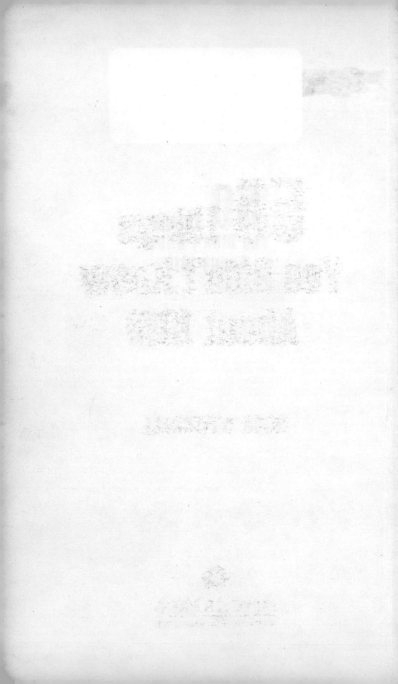

50 Things You Didn't Know About 1916

MICK O'FARRELL

MERCIER PRESS
IRISH PUBLISHER – IRISH STORY

MERCIER PRESS

Cork

www.mercierpress.ie

Trade enquiries to CMD,
55A Spruce Avenue, Stillorgan Industrial Park,
Blackrock, County Dublin

© Mick O'Farrell, 2009

ISBN: 978 1 85635 619 0

10 9 8 7 6 5 4 3 2 1

A CIP record for this title is available from the British
Library

 Mercier Press receives financial assistance from
the Arts Council/An Chomhairle Ealaíon

Printed and bound in the EU.

For three generations of O'Farrell women, Amanda (née Edwards), Eve and Ursula, who each provide support, inspiration and love in their own way: subtle and obvious, intended and unintended, consciously and unconsciously.

Contents

Acknowledgements		10
Introduction		11
1	Looking the other way	15
2	A big what-if? Well, not quite ...	17
3	First shot of the Rising?	20
4	The rebellion's first casualties	22
5	From Kaiser to Kilcoole	24
6	'Flintlocks, shotguns and elephant rifles, as well as more orthodox weapons'	27
7	Travelling to rebellion I	30
8	The return of looted goods	33
9	To France ... via Dublin	35
10	In harm's way – deliberately	36
11	Travelling to rebellion II	40
12	A ceasefire for ducks	43
13	Galway coastal shelling	45
14	Rebels on bicycles	47
15	Brothers in arms I	50

16	World's first ever radio broadcast	53
17	Receipts – official and unofficial politeness	56
18	Today's rebels – yesterday's Olympians	60
19	A crack shot in TCD	63
20	What was life like for a rebel under fire?	65
21	What did Bella Glockler think?	69
22	Duelling snipers	73
23	Ruling the waves	76
24	Boy soldiers	79
25	Foreign fighters	81
26	Small memories, big impact	84
27	Delivering soldiers instead of stout	88
28	Mobile marine artillery	92
29	Brothers in arms II	94
30	Skeffy's companions in death	96
31	Deadly rooftops	100
32	Bodies buried and bodies burned	102
33	Testing times indeed	105
34	Sackville Street or O'Connell Street?	107
35	Lenin looks on	110

36	'It wasn't Sinn Féin made the Rising – 'twas the Rising made Sinn Féin'	112
37	From British gunboat to Irish patrol vessel	115
38	Scars in stone and statue	117
39	Scars in wood	120
40	Scars in paper	122
41	Executing his orders	124
42	Lucky escapes	127
43	From broadcasting rebel to Quiet Man	130
44	From Dublin to Hollywood	132
45	Dublin Mean Time vs Greenwich Mean Time	134
46	Who's going to pay for all this?	135
47	Rebellion's silver lining	138
48	Final shots ...	141
49	How hot off the presses?	143
50	And finally ...	145
Endnotes		149
Bibliography		154

Acknowledgements

Many thanks to the following for providing information and, in some cases, material: Ursula O'Farrell; Jimmy McDonagh; Derek Jones; Douglas S. Appleyard; John McGuiggan; Sarah McLoughlin; Karl Vines; Nick Goad; Michael J. Murray, TCD; Amanda Hyland, Laois County Library; Muriel McCarthy, Marsh's Library; Andrew Hesketh, www.derbyshirelads.uwclub.net; Very Rev. Patrick Finn, St Mary's, Haddington Road. Thanks also to Eoin Purcell and the team at Mercier Press for taking me on – again.

Note: Every effort has been made to acknowledge the sources of all photographs used. Should a source not have been acknowledged, please contact Mercier Press and we will make the necessary corrections at the first opportunity.

Introduction

I've been a student of the Easter Rising for a long time now, and in that time I've learned many things. When my interest in the rebellion began, I used to think that since, at a very basic level, the Rising started and ended within a single week, it would be a finite area of study. How wrong I was! Fifteen years of reading and researching later, I'm still experiencing the pleasure of learning new things, finding new unpublished sources, and chasing scarce publications. And yet there remains much more out there – many facts waiting to be uncovered and connections waiting to be made.

There are, of course, some facts about the Easter Rising that are fairly widely known. Not everybody knows the details of that week in 1916, but a lot of people would know a little, and a few people would know a lot. This book is an attempt at presenting some of the many less well-known facts about the Rising and, as such, I hope it is of interest to people at all levels of knowledge. I don't mind admitting that I found out a few new things myself during my research!

The truth of it is that no matter how long a person spends reading and researching the Rising, many tales and facts will never be revealed – things said in secret, acts of courage or cowardice unwitnessed, tales told to family and friends, never committed to paper and now lost, tales untold by men who saw, or perhaps did, things they chose not to recall.

All memories are fleeting, though, and if history is to be known to more than historians, then it is up to all of us to tell, to listen, to preserve – how many of us have heard stories of times past and said we must write that down some day; only to try and tell the same story to a new audience and have trouble remembering this detail, or that name?

So if you have, or have heard, a family story about the Easter Rising (or any other historical event) write it down – scribble it, type it, email it to yourself! Anything to keep it – for yourself, for the next generation, for historians and non-historians. And if retaining it is a burden, send it to me, and I'll keep it for you!

When it comes to history, we can all look up the big events, the important dates, if we want to, in any number of books. But what interests me more are the so-called ordinary stories, the tales of the unimportant. What was it like to hear gunfire on Easter Monday and worry about getting enough bread the next day? What was it like to board a troop ship in Liverpool in the middle of the night, bound for who-knows-where, only to land in the unfamiliar port of Kingstown (Dun Laoghaire), to be cheered as you disembarked and to be shot at as you arrived in Mount Street? How did it feel to have your windows blown in by the booming of the artillery which the army was firing from outside your home?

Ordinary people lived through these extraordinary times and their tales deserve to be known, to be remembered, to be told.

Here then, are some extraordinarily ordinary, but fascinating, facts about the Easter Rising which you may not have known before now.

Mick O'Farrell
December 2008

Author's Notes: apart from some small actions, the 1916 Rising lasted seven days, from Easter Monday, 24 April, to the following Sunday, 30 April. Therefore, when the text mentions a day, without giving a date, it can be assumed that the day referred to is one of the seven days between that Monday and Sunday.

The 'old' and 'new' name of Sackville/O'Connell Street are used throughout the text – Fact 34 explains why both names were valid in 1916.

1

Looking the other way

To help the success of the Rising, the Volunteer leaders sought help from Britain's enemy, Germany, in more ways than one – there was the well-known arms shipment carried by the disguised vessel, the *Aud*, which ended up scuttled at the bottom of the sea (*see Fact 2*). There was also the failed attempt by Roger Casement to establish an Irish Brigade from among Irishmen held prisoner in Germany.

In general, however, the German reaction was best described as lukewarm – they flatly refused requests to land troops in Ireland and said that sending submarines into Dublin harbour was impossible. And although they did send a single arms shipment, it comprised weapons previously captured from the Russians and of debatable quality – 'the rifles, which had been deemed good enough for Sinn Féiners, were by no means modern', was one description.[1]

Nevertheless, a less well-known German effort in support of the rebellion took place early on Tuesday morning – this was the diversionary naval shelling of the English coastal towns of Yarmouth and Lowestoft. 'No doubt,' according to a dispatch from Commander-in-Chief, Field-Marshal French, 'the object of this demonstration was to assist the Irish rebellion and to distract attention from Ireland'.

Even this supporting action, however, could be described as lukewarm. Despite involving more than four German battle cruisers and six light cruisers, the whole event lasted less than an hour – the bombardment of Lowestoft lasted just ten minutes and that of Yarmouth only a couple of minutes. The Germans were then engaged by a British naval force and, according to Field-Marshal French, the German shelling 'failed entirely to accomplish its object'. *The Irish Times* reported that the raid was marked 'by ineffective shooting and other instances of extreme nervousness and haste'.

Nevertheless, despite failing to distract attention from Ireland, the raid's 'ineffective shooting' resulted in about 200 houses destroyed, as well as the deaths of two men, one woman and a child.

2 A big what-if? Well, not quite ...

One widely-known fact about the Rising has led, over the years, to one of the most commonly-asked 'What if ...' questions.

As outlined in Fact 1, one of the few practical offers of help that the German government made to the rebels was the dispatch of an arms shipment on board the *Libau*, disguised to look like the neutral Norwegian *Aud*. Intercepted by the British Navy in Tralee Bay, the *Aud*'s captain, Lieutenant Karl Spindler, tried various ruses to get away, but a shot fired across the bows of the ship finally halted him. Spindler agreed to follow his escort to Queenstown (Cobh) harbour, but having travelled some distance, he halted unexpectedly. The 'Norwegian' crew, now dressed in German naval uniform, began abandoning ship into lowered lifeboats. Charges had been laid in the *Aud*'s hold, an explosion rang out, and the ship sank within ten minutes. Gone was her cargo of 20,000 rifles, ten machine guns, and one million rounds of ammunition, all of which, although of debatable quality, could have made an enormous difference to the outcome of the rebellion.

And that raised the question which has so often been asked since then – what if the *Aud*'s cargo had been successfully landed and the arms had spread out into the countryside as planned?

There are several well-known reasons for the *Aud*'s failure to deliver its cargo, including a change of rendezvous dates which wasn't communicated to the crew and the accidental drowning of the Volunteers sent to meet the boat.

However, the hard fact is that the *Aud*'s mission to deliver guns to the Volunteers was always doomed to fail and there never was an alternative outcome.

During the First World War, the boffins of British naval intelligence were based in a single room, Room 40, in the Old Building of the Admiralty (their room number became their nickname). Because of their earlier code-breaking successes, the team in Room 40 knew about the voyage of the *Aud* almost before she had left port. Indeed, the navy had been expecting an attempt at gun-running for quite a while – for more than six weeks before the *Aud* even set sail, Admiral Sir Lewis Bayly, Commander-in-Chief, Coast of Ireland, had ordered a number of ships to patrol the west coast with the specific aim of intercepting any vessels acting suspiciously. In the *Aud*'s first two encounters with these ships, Spindler's disguise worked well, but it was only a matter of time before her luck ran out.

So in fact there is no need to ponder what might have happened if the *Aud*'s cargo of guns and ammunition had made it to dry land, because the 'what if ...' scenario could never actually have happened. It wasn't bad luck, bad timing, or bad organisation that led to the *Aud*'s scuttling, it was the inevitable result of dedicated code-breaking by Room 40, a 'band of professors, clergymen, actors, art experts and naval officers' who mastered Germany's codes and affected the course of not just the First World War, but also Ireland's Easter rebellion.

3

First shot of the Rising?

Unsurprisingly, the first shot of the Rising has more than one claimant. However, one claim that has many supporters is that of the Volunteers of Laois, who destroyed a section of railway track at a place called Colt Wood on the night of 23 April – the day before the Rising began in Dublin.

A monument to the event was erected near Colt Wood in 1996, in an area called Clonadadoran, on the N8 between Portlaoise and Abbeyleix. The monument bears three plaques – a copy of the Proclamation, a picture of a derailed train and a dedication, which names the Volunteers and reads:

First Shot in 1916 Rising

On Easter Sunday night, 23rd April, 1916, acting under the direct orders of Patrick Pearse, the Laois Volunteers participated in the demolition of a section of the Abbeyleix-Portlaoise railway line at a location near here.

The purpose of this exercise was to prevent British military reinforcements from reaching Dublin via Waterford after the Rising had started. This demolition was followed by the firing of the first shot of the 1916 Rising.

Other activities engaged in by the Laois Volunteers included an attempted similar demolition of the Carlow-Kildare railway line and a raid on the Wolfhill RIC Barracks.[1]

Amazingly, the raid on the Wolfhill RIC Barracks was carried out by a single Volunteer, John Frawley, who attacked the Barracks alone. The details of this raid are not known, but Frawley's name appears on the prisoner's lists in the *Sinn Féin Rebellion Handbook*.

4 The rebellion's first casualties

Although (unbeknownst to themselves) the rebels had some success with telegraphy during Easter Week (*see Fact 16*), an earlier mission involving Volunteer and wireless expert Con Keating proved not only less successful, but in fact fatal.

On the morning of Good Friday, three days before the Rising began, five men were ordered by the rebel leaders to travel by train to Killarney in County Kerry, where they were to be met by two cars which would bring them to Caherciveen. The mission's aim was to dismantle the wireless station at Caherciveen, re-assemble it in Tralee and try to contact the ship carrying arms from Germany (*see Fact 2*).

Although they started out in good weather, by the time the cars reached Killorglin 'the night had turned very murky'.[1] At some point in the journey, the two cars became separated, and when the first one was within a few miles of Caherciveen, it stopped and the men waited. But the second car never arrived.

Tragically, having taken a wrong turn in Killorglin, the

second car was unwittingly heading for nearby Ballykissane pier and it drove straight into the freezing cold water of the River Laune. The driver, Tommy MacInerney, managed to get out, as did Con Keating. Having swum together for a few minutes, MacInerney heard Keating say 'Jesus, Mary and Joseph', before sinking out of sight. The other two passengers, Donal Sheehan and Charles Monaghan, also drowned, but MacInerney was eventually guided to shore by a local. Keating and Sheehan's bodies were recovered the next day, but Monaghan's remains weren't found until six months later.

These three men were the first casualties of the Easter Rising, and, as it turns out, their deaths were utterly pointless because, as we now know with the benefit of hindsight, the German arms ship had already been at the Kerry coast and, unable to make contact with the shore, had gone. Moreover, not only was the ship no longer at the rendezvous point, but in fact it didn't even have a wireless on board to begin with.

5

From Kaiser to Kilcoole

The 'standard' weapon used by the rebels during the Rising was the Mauser Model 1871/84 single shot 11mm rifle. In 1914, 1,500 of these weapons were purchased in Germany on behalf of the Volunteers and landed in Ireland, along with 45,000 rounds of ammunition.

Heavy and cumbersome though they were, the Mauser was a very efficient weapon in the right hands – for snipers, it was 'a really excellent weapon'.[1] For the inexperienced, though, firing one for the first time could be a risky business: Volunteer Tom Walsh at Mount Street Bridge was knocked unconscious by the recoil of his first shot.

An unexpected advantage of the rifle's calibre was its booming sound – a 'low roar' – which made it sound like distant artillery, especially when several were fired at once. This made it difficult for the British to know how well armed the rebels might in fact be.

However, for the most part, the 'importing' of the Mausers in 1914 is a story that is only half known. What is well known is that many of the rifles were initially landed at Howth, County Dublin, during a daylight operation on

26 July. Having landed the arms, the Volunteers started back to Dublin with them, but were intercepted by the Dublin Metropolitan Police and about 150 soldiers of the King's Own Scottish Borderers. A small number of Volunteers kept the authorities talking while the rest disappeared with the weapons. As a result, while marching back to their barracks, the soldiers were subjected to harassment and jeering, until finally on Bachelor's Walk they opened fire on the crowd. Four civilians died and the incident became known as the Bachelor's Walk Massacre; the troops were thenceforth jeeringly referred to as the King's Own Scottish Murderers.

Meanwhile, the rifles themselves became popularly known as 'Howth Mausers', and indeed, so glad were many rebels to finally have a weapon and so attached to them did they become, that a song was written about them, called *My Old Howth Gun*, which included the lines:

> In Ireland's day of need,
> Ah you proved a friend indeed
> When you made the bullet speed
> O me old Howth gun.

However, the consignment of Mausers was, in fact, landed at two locations: one was obviously Howth, but the other less well-known landing point was Kilcoole, County Wicklow, on 1 August.

That night, a steam yacht called the *Chotah* manoeuvred as close to the beach as possible, where it was met by several smaller boats. The rifles and ammunition were transferred to these boats and then brought to shore. There they were met by Volunteers who waded in, took the cargo and loaded it onto a waiting convoy of three lorries, six cars and twelve motorbikes with sidecars.

By 3 a.m., the operation had passed off fairly smoothly (including the temporary detention of two inquisitive Royal Irish Constables) and the *Chotah* sailed away. Then, shouldering any weapons that weren't loaded onto the vehicles, the Volunteers formed up on the beach and marched to Kilcoole village, singing *A Nation Once Again* and *God Save Ireland*.

Having been released, meanwhile, the two constables tried to raise the alarm, only to find that communications had been cut. Eventually, having catching the 3.30 a.m. train to Bray, one of them managed to get the word out, but by then the rifles and ammunition had already reached Dublin and were being distributed to Volunteer units across the city.

6

'Flintlocks, shotguns and elephant rifles, as well as more orthodox weapons'

In any uprising against officialdom, it is unsurprising that a would-be rebel will make use of whatever weapon is available, but the sheer variety of offensive implements used by insurgents during the Easter Rising might surprise readers.

Of course, thousands of weapons were shipped to Ireland from overseas – 1,500 German Mauser rifles were landed successfully at Howth and Kilcoole in 1914 (*see Fact 5*), but another 20,000 rifles went to the bottom of the sea in 1916 (*see Fact 2*).

Many other rifles were bought legitimately by individual Volunteers and Citizen Army men (some even won in raffles), and an unknown number of English-made Lee-Enfield rifles were bought, bartered or stolen from British soldiers and police barracks around the country. Other rifles carried by rebels included Italian Martinis, English Lee-Metfords and Sniders. There were also numbers of shotguns, some of them American, which apparently had 'an unlucky knack of going off on their own'.

These were the 'orthodox weapons', but there were many unorthodox weapons put to use in 1916. On a big table in the GPO, 'a large array of daggers, bayonets and many weird varieties of lethal weapons were laid out'. There were also bombs 'made out of condensed milk tins, jam jars [and] lengths of piping'.[1] Captain Arthur Dickson (*see Fact 40*) described his first action in Dublin as 'a baptism of fire … with flintlocks, shotguns and elephant rifles, as well as more orthodox weapons'.

Harking back to rebellions of previous generations, the pike made a reappearance on the streets of Dublin – without rifles to shoulder, many Volunteers began the rebellion carrying nothing more than a weapon which wouldn't have looked out of place on a medieval battlefield. Yet however archaic they were, the pikes were still better than nothing, and in a close-up situation, cold steel will always carry some authority.

On his way into the GPO on Easter Monday, Second Lieutenant A.D. Chalmers saw the rebels marching in formation along O'Connell Street and remarked 'Just look at that awful crowd!'[2] Within minutes, the 'awful crowd' had rushed inside the GPO with rebellion on their minds and Chalmers was staring at the pointed end of a pike (he was held prisoner until Friday, when the building was evacuated).

In another incident, Volunteer Andy McDonnell was

ordered to hold up a tram, and so, armed only with a six-foot pike, he stood in the street with his pike 'at the ready'. Ready for what, he never had to discover, since, 'to my great relief' the tram in fact halted.[3]

Interestingly though, the use of the pike, in the absence of more orthodox weapons, wasn't just confined to the rebels. When the threat of attack on Trinity College spurred the staff into action, one of them, Chief Steward Joseph Marshall, might have been forgiven for experiencing a sense of déjà vu. Marshall had been a constable with the Dublin Metropolitan Police during the Fenian rising of 1867, during which time he had seized a number of rebel pikes. Now, nearly fifty years later, after ordering that the college's front gate be closed and padlocked, Marshall distributed those same pikes to his staff, to be used as a defence against the 'Fenians' ideological descendants'.[4]

7
Travelling to rebellion I

Rebels arrived for duty on Easter Monday in ones and twos, by various means – on foot, by bicycle, or by public transport. At least one even arrived by automobile (*see Fact 11*).

However, one body of rebels travelled to O'Connell Street *en masse*. These were the so-called Kimmage men, a group of Irishmen and would-be rebels who had been living and working abroad, but who had come to Dublin from cities across Great Britain after the introduction of conscription. Staying at 'Larkfield', the Kimmage farm of Count Plunkett (father of rebel leader Joseph Plunkett), the men lived together in a derelict flour mill on the property for three months before the Rising began.

There they set up a drill hall and a shooting range, and slept on bags of straw on hard boards. At night they went on route marches and, when they weren't drilling, they spent their days making crude pikes and filling shotgun cartridges with home-made pellets. Up to 5,000 pellets a day were produced from scrap lead and when enough material was available, hand grenades were produced.

In this way, many Volunteer units were supplied with ammunition in the lead-up to the rebellion.

When the day of rebellion finally dawned, the Kimmage men were ready and eager to get going. The company marched to the nearby tram line and boarded a tram, each of them carrying not just a rifle or shotgun, but 'a spare pike' and other equipment as well.[1] Despite all the hardware, somehow they got themselves onto the tram, and, rebellion notwithstanding, paid their fares – '59 twopenny fares' requested their captain, George Plunkett, of the conductor, 'and please don't stop until we reach O'Connell Bridge.'

'Why bother to pay anyway,' was the reply, 'when you've already captured the tram?'

Volunteer James Brennan helped proceedings along by prodding the conductor with his shotgun.

Some of the discomfited civilians protested, one shouting to the conductor: 'I demand that you put these men off!'

To which he replied: 'Would you mind doing it yourself, ma'am. As you can see, I'm rather busy.'[2]

Volunteer Joe Good remembered that it was a warm sunny day and the rebels 'were as cheerful as excursionists off to the seaside'. Johnny 'Blimey' O'Connor played a flute and 'we sang on the top of the open tram. We were jeered at, and cheered back at travellers on the trams passing in the opposite direction.'[3] From O'Connell Street, the men moved to muster outside Liberty Hall, before returning to O'Connell Street via Abbey Street and ultimately occupying the GPO.

As some of the more committed men to fight during the rebellion, the Kimmage Garrison acquitted itself well, but at a cost. In his memoirs, Joe Good remarked that the Kimmage men were referred to as 'George's lambs' by the other Plunketts: 'Perhaps they named us well, for he led us to the slaughter.'

8

The return of looted goods

As O'Connell Street and the surrounding area emptied of policemen, it didn't take long for the vacuum of authority to be filled by the anarchy of the mob. 'The Government had mysteriously vanished,' wrote one observer.[1] Looting began early in the week, and didn't stop until the fires which eventually consumed much of the area had taken hold.

Tales of looting outside the O'Connell Street area are fairly uncommon, but there are enough well-known stories of looting within that area to fill a lot of pages – like the bare-footed boy with an armful of expensive boots, who was stopped by a priest demanding to know where he'd got them. 'In Earl Street, Father,' came the reply, 'but you have to hurry up or they'll all be gone.'[2]

Meanwhile, author St John G. Ervine wrote of a looter who 'went into an abandoned tram-car [and] stripped his rags off … When he reappeared, swaggering up and down the street, he was wearing brown boots, a dress-suit, a Panama hat and carrying a lady's sunshade.'

However, embarrassed by the dishonourable carry-on of their fellow citizens, the rebels tried many times and in many ways to stop the looting – from pouring water on them to firing over their heads, all to no avail. And wherever looting took place, fires soon followed, reducing much of O'Connell Street to charred ruins.

One aspect of the looting which is less well known, is the attempt made to seek the return of looted goods. Eva Fay was living in a tenement in Hardwicke Place (known as George's Pocket, beside St George's church) in 1916, and soon after the rebellion began, a drapery called Baker and Sons on the corner of Dorset Street 'had its windows smashed, and some drapery goods were carried off by looters'.[3] Among the goods were suits, which were brought to the nearby flats, where the enterprising looters sold them, Eva's mother being one of the buyers.

Next day, however, armed men, possibly Volunteers, arrived on a mission to retrieve the looted goods and return them to their owners, and one of the flats they searched was Eva's. But the word had gone around in advance of the men's arrival and the precious suit was hidden up the chimney and remained there undiscovered – a dishonourable carry-on perhaps, but if we lived in a five-storey tenement with no running water, a shared toilet in the backyard and thirteen children (only four of whom survived to adulthood), which of us might not be tempted to do the same thing?

9

To France ... via Dublin

When the rebel shooting began, the British authorities were taken by surprise, but, after a short hesitation, the machinery of empire swung into action and troops and artillery were quickly on their way to suppress the insurrection.

Apart from reinforcements sent from within the island of Ireland itself (from Athlone, the Curragh Camp in Kildare, Templemore and Belfast), troops were also urgently sent from England, many of whom were less than three months in uniform. However, the men moved more quickly than did the news of their destination, with the result that many soldiers landed in Dun Laoghaire harbour, thinking they were in France.

One journalist wrote: 'The troops ... did not know where they were. One asked me if he was at Le Havre. Most of them thought they were in France. One was going to send a postcard home from "Somewhere in France" 'til he got enlightened.'[1]

10 In harm's way – deliberately

When reading about the rebellion, it is easy sometimes to imagine that when the shooting began, the streets would have emptied, leaving only the rebels and the British army to fight it out, with the odd gathering of looters here and there.

In fact, in the early days of Easter Week, the streets were busy, because, apart from combatants and bullets, there were large numbers of civilians out and about – not frightened civilians rushing to safety, but sightseers moving here and there, trying to get a look at the action. On some occasions they were out in great numbers and at all times they were in great danger.

We might find that a hard fact to believe these days, that civilians would put themselves in danger's way just to see what was happening, but in 1916 there were no on-the-spot reporters for radio, let alone TV. With even the newspapers out of circulation for most of Easter Week, getting on to the streets and finding out the facts for themselves was the direct method chosen by a lot of citizens eager to know what was happening.

The result was that crowds gathered at junctions and street corners, some even shouting advice. 'We all began to cheer and wave our hats and shout orders to the soldiers: "Go round the back ... ye'll be shot dead!"' wrote one by-stander.[1]

On O'Connell Street a large crowd of people were massed in front of the GPO. Soon a large number of priests arrived, and, having failed to persuade the crowd to go home, 'the clergymen formed a line across the street and began to try to push the people back ... but as they pressed one lot backwards another crowd began to form up in the space they had cleared. Turning patiently, the clergy began to push the new crowd back ... only to discover that the old crowd began to follow them.'[2]

Meanwhile Volunteers bringing commandeered provisions into the GPO were 'struggling to get into the building through milling crowds of onlookers'.[3]

Just after the occupation of the GPO, a witness noted 'the cheering of the crowd, though this was very insignificant and in no way represented any considerable body of citizens, any of the better class having disappeared, leaving the streets to idlers and women and children or else stray sightseers.'[4]

Sightseeing wasn't just centred on O'Connell Street either. At Mount Street Bridge, even during the fighting, a witness noted 'a mass of civilian spectators up to within

50 yards of [the soldiers] and directly in front, blocking the street'.[5] Of himself he said: 'For half an hour or so I was a passive spectator, though intensely interested by the sight of a real battle going on under my very eyes at a distance hardly more than that of the gallery from a large music-hall stage.'

Meanwhile, a British army officer's wife wrote that her friend Nettie watered her garden 'to the cheery accompaniment of whizzing bullets'.[6]

In his seminal book on 1916, Max Caulfield wrote that in the pause before a British attack on a rebel outpost 'civilians, sensing an entertainment, huddled close to the walls in Dame Street or crouched in shop doorways'. When the attack began, 'the effect on the crowd was comical. Men darted away like rabbits, women fainted. Some people in their panic ran straight into the firing line, causing a sudden ceasefire, and the combatants shouted at them angrily from the rooftops.'

Unfortunately, but unsurprisingly, with so many non-combatats milling around, there were inevitably civilian casualties. One history of the Rising gives figures of 450 people killed and 2,614 wounded. Of the dead, 116 are listed as military, 16 policemen and, unable to a large degree to distinguish between civilian and rebel, the author simply lists 318 others. However, other records say that 64 rebels died during the fighting, so we can say that about 254 non-combatants died during the week. Among civilians/rebels, there were also 2,217 wounded.

While some of the civilian victims remain nameless to this day, there are many accounts of how individuals met their deaths. For instance, on O'Connell Street, a witness told of how: 'The street was empty except for one man … wearing a top hat and frock coat … trying to take cover, but suddenly, as I watched there was a shot. The man in the frock coat sagged, stiffened and went down on his knees. There he remained in that curious attitude for two days.'[7]

Also on O'Connell Street, a Volunteer watched as a blind man made his way along the road, with his white stick in front of him. A sniper fired and the man fell. A St John's Ambulance man ran to bandage him and help him up, but as the pair made their way across the bridge, the sniper fired twice more and both men fell dead.

Back in the Mount Street area, there were many civilian casualties – in one case a single bullet entered and killed one woman, before exiting and then wounding her daughter; in another case, an eyewitness saw a Mr Charles Hayter, a seventy-seven-year-old grocer from Northumberland Road, 'foolishly dart into the road and get himself killed'.[8] Subsequently, in 1917, his widow, Mrs Mary Ann Hayter, was awarded £150 in compensation.

11 Travelling to rebellion II

Not many rebels drove to the rebellion in style, but The O'Rahilly was the exception – he arrived at the muster point outside Liberty Hall on Easter Monday in a French De Dion Bouton automobile, laden with rifles.

The O'Rahilly was director of arms for the Irish Volunteers, and in fact he'd spent much of the weekend driving around the countryside spreading Volunteer President Eoin MacNeill's countermanding order, the aim of which was to prevent a rebellion. However, when he discovered that the Rising was going ahead in any case, The O'Rahilly joined the insurgents without hesitation. One of the Kimmage men (*see Fact 7*) overheard him say: 'I helped wind this clock and I've come to hear it strike.'[1]

The four-cylinder De Dion Bouton was owned jointly by The O'Rahilly and his sister Anna, who each paid £200 for it around 1911. The car's body was built in Dublin by O'Grady's coachbuilders of Dawson Street.

Anna was with The O'Rahilly when he arrived at Liberty Hall and went into the building with her brother and the other rebel leaders. She went over to Pearse, pinched his arm to get his attention and said: 'This is all your fault'. Anna had intended to drive the car home after the weapons had been unloaded, but she was asked to leave it behind as transport for the rebel forces and she walked home – she would never drive the De Dion Bouton again.

The car was subsequently used to transport rifles, tools and homemade bombs to the GPO and then left outside the building on Prince's Street, probably as part of a barricade. However, after the fires that swept O'Connell Street had been put out, all that was left of The O'Rahilly's prized car was a burnt-out shell, and when Dublin corporation were clearing the rubble from the street, they sent a note to his wife, asking her how she wanted it disposed of. Her son Aodogán later wrote: 'At the time no one thought it would be an interesting souvenir of the Rising and Nannie told them to dump it.'[2] The debris from O'Connell Street was in fact then used to form Hill 16 in Croke Park, and the remains of the De Dion Bouton probably found their final resting place there.

Meanwhile, The O'Rahilly's final resting place turned out to be a lane near the GPO, where he died having been wounded while leading an attack on a British barricade on Moore Street. Lying in the lane and knowing he was dying, he wrote a final note to his wife on the back of a piece of paper on which his son had written a note to him earlier in the week. 'I got more than one bullet I think,' he wrote and, indeed, the paper itself had been pierced by a bullet. Then, in a final dramatic gesture, The O'Rahilly used his own blood to write on the doorway beside him: 'Here died The O'Rahilly RIP.' The lane he died in is now called O'Rahilly Parade.

12 A ceasefire for ducks

One of the first acts by the Irish Citizen Army in the Rising was to occupy St Stephen's Green, a strategically important location because a number of main routes into the city crossed through, or near, the Green. So, along with a number of Volunteers, the ICA marched up Grafton Street, entered the park, ordered civilians to leave and took prisoner any off-duty soldiers unlucky enough to be present.

However, with so many large buildings overlooking the Green (including the Shelbourne Hotel) and not enough men to occupy a useful number of them, the rebels' position in the Green rapidly became untenable. British forces swept the Green with gunfire, particularly from the windows of the Shelbourne, and the rebels were forced to withdraw to the Royal College of Surgeons – losing one man as they dashed across the road.

In contrast, things weren't so bad for the park's feathered inhabitants. *The Times History of the War* reported soon after the rebellion that St Stephen's Green 'was well stocked with waterfowl, and the keeper, who remained inside all the time, reported that his charges were well looked after and fed by him, and were very little perturbed by the bullets flying over their heads'.

The park-keeper's name was Mr James Kearney – every day he would leave his house in the Green to feed the ducks, and every day the opposing sides would cease firing to allow him to do so.

13 Galway coastal shelling

Although Dublin was the main centre of 'activity' during the week of the rebellion, some unrest was evident around the country. However, with various on-again, off-again messages being delivered to rebel leaders, confusion inevitably reigned. Communication was a lot more difficult in those days and, in some instances, instructions cancelling one set of orders were received well before the original orders themselves were delivered.

Nevertheless, County Galway was one area which saw a large band of rebels assemble, ready for action, under leader Liam Mellows. Around 1,000 Volunteers reported for duty and, despite a crippling lack of arms (one report says that there wasn't more than 120 rifles and shotguns between them all), detachments carried out some raids and ambushes, taking several policemen prisoner.

It wasn't just in numbers of guns that the Galway rebels were lacking though, it was in sheer calibre that they were literally outgunned. On Wednesday morning, the *HMS Laburnum* arrived in Galway Bay and that afternoon, when some cars were seen approaching Galway city, the

Laburnum opened fire. Directed by an observer on land, the sloop's log for 26 April records: 'Fired nine rounds from after gun in direction of rebels advancing on Galway town, 2.30 p.m.'

However, despite there being some doubt as to who was actually in the cars (Mellows hadn't ordered any advance on Galway), the booming of naval artillery had a definite negative effect on rebel morale. C. Desmond Greaves wrote that 'No better explanation has been offered than that it was intended to frighten the rebels and cheer the loyalists ... They must have felt highly reassured when they heard the Navy banging away.'[1]

14 Rebels on bicycles

Movement around the city of Dublin was difficult under fire, and no doubt it seemed a good idea to present a faster-moving target through the use of bicycles. These were employed for carrying dispatches and for 'hit and run' sorties. However, despite the advantage of increased speed, in at least two instances, bands of rebels travelling on bicycles met with fatal results.

On the first day of the rebellion, three rebel cyclists were fired on by Anzac marksmen, as they passed Trinity College, and two were hit. One escaped, wounded, on foot, but the other, Gerald Keogh, was killed – an eyewitness with the garrison inside the college recalled: 'It was wonderful shooting … Four shots were fired. Three found their mark in the head of the unfortunate victim.'[1] The body was taken into the Provost's House and lay in an empty room for three days, before, remaining unclaimed, it was buried temporarily in College Park (*see Fact 32*).

Another rebel patrol on bicycles which ended in disaster occurred when a party of men from the garrison in Jacob's factory (now the Dublin Institute of Technology) were selected for a sortie to relieve the pressure on the Volunteers holding Westland Row railway station and Boland's Mills. In his statement to the Bureau of Military History in 1949, Volunteer Seosamh de Brún wrote that Commandant Thomas MacDonagh told every man to select a bicycle from a heap of machines nearby. 'I happened to select a first class one with a rifle holder ...' Before setting out, however, one of the twenty or so men suggested a cup of tea and 'the Commandant acquiesced'.

The cycle from Jacob's to Merrion Square proceeded without incident, but then suddenly the rebels came under fire from 'khaki-clad men [who] dropped to their knees and blazed away'. The cyclists sought whatever cover was available, before deciding to cut short their mission and head back to Jacob's. They returned by a different route and this time came under heavy fire from the top of Grafton Street.

'A breeze of bullets whizzed by us', de Brún wrote, but luckily the rebels in the College of Surgeons provided some covering fire. However, one man, Volunteer John O'Grady, was hit and, despite being taken back to Jacob's and the Adelaide Hospital for treatment, he died of his wounds.

Interestingly, in contrast to his 'on the spot' diary (*see Fact 20*), which states that the sortie happened on Saturday, de Brún's statement to the Bureau records it as happening on Friday. Meanwhile, the statements of some of his fellow Jacob's rebels offer further confusion. For instance, Volunteer Michael Walker (*see Fact 18*) in his 1948 statement to the Bureau, initially put the sortie as occurring on Wednesday – this was then crossed out and Thursday inserted instead. An article in the 1966 *Capuchin Annual* also says the cyclists set out on Thursday. However, the caretaker of Jacob's factory, Thomas Orr, states that the sortie did indeed take place on Saturday.

All of which provides a perfect example of how an historian's primary sources can't always be relied on as 100 per cent accurate. In this instance, however, since de Brún's diary was written at the time, it must surely give the correct day for the bicycle sortie, Saturday, since the sources which disagree were compiled long after the event – in de Brún's own case, thirty-six years later.

15 Brothers in arms I

One of today's main sources of information on many aspects of the Rising is the *Sinn Féin Rebellion Handbook*, originally published in 1916 by the *Weekly Irish Times*. Of course, given the paper's pro-union stance then, as well as the short time between the events and the book's publication, the *Handbook* isn't 100 per cent reliable as a source, particularly when opinion leaks into historical reporting.

However, when it comes to hard facts, such as lists of casualties, prisoners and medal recipients, the *Handbook* is very useful (although not necessarily complete).

One section of the book, *Prisoners Deported and Released*, includes lists of prisoners processed in Richmond Barracks in Dublin up to 11 July, 1916 – 3,149 men and 77 women, of which 1,852 men and 5 women were deported to prisons up and down the UK.

An interesting fact which emerges from a review of these lists, is the remarkable number of detainees who were literally brothers in arms (or fathers and sons in arms). Picking out names which share the same address, there are

103 pairs and 15 triples, and in the case of the McHughs of 115 James' Street, William, Miles, Edward and Patrick were all together when 'received at Wakefield Detention Barracks on May 6th'.

Checking the McHughs on the 1911 Dublin census, we find that in 1916, William could have been either the family's father at age fifty-three, or the youngest son at age sixteen. Edward (25), Miles (22), and Patrick (20) were all brothers. (Interestingly, at least five other prisoners gave the same address, of 115 James' Street, including a pair of Gibsons.)

But the *Handbook* doesn't provide the whole story – for instance, a well-known pair of brothers that don't appear are Garry and Paddy Holohan, who took part in an attack on the Magazine Fort in Phoenix Park. In another example, two brothers, Michael and John Edwards, are listed, but since they fought in different areas, they appear in different lists, Michael being sent to Stafford and John to Knutsford.

The Edwards brothers also illustrate another aspect of the make-up of the Volunteers – the numbers that came from the same urban areas. When Michael and John left their house in 25 St Michael's Terrace, Blackpitts, Dublin 8, to fight in the rebellion, accompanying them from the same street were P. O'Brien from No. 26, Edward Gibson from No. 31 and Jas McGuire from No. 32.

Meanwhile, Seán O'Mahony's book *Frongoch*, which gives a history of the internment camp in Wales where the Irish detainees were eventually gathered together, also contains lists of prisoners assembled from the prisoners' camp register. An examination of this list shows 111 pairs, 22 triples and 10 possible quadruples.

However, while this kind of analysis can provide an overall picture, it can never be precise, and neither source claims to be complete – indeed, the McHughs don't feature in the *Frongoch* list at all and presumably were never brought there!

There were also, of course, several 'famous' pairs of brothers who, for various reasons, including execution, don't appear on any prisoner lists: Patrick and Willie Pearse, Michael and Henry O'Hanrahan, and Thomas, David and Richard Kent (*see Fact 48*).

16 World's first ever radio broadcast

In 1916 wireless communication was in its infancy and, in general, signals were targeted to particular receiving stations. The idea that a signal might be broadcast into the atmosphere in the hopes that someone might pick it up was a fairly radical one – there was, of course, a commercially used wavelength for shipping, but it was only for communication at sea.

On the afternoon of Easter Monday, rebel leader Joseph Plunkett sent seven men from the GPO across O'Connell Street to occupy the Wireless School of Telegraphy which had been shut down and sealed by the authorities at the start of the First World War and the equipment dismantled.

One of the seven rebels was Fergus O'Kelly, who had served with the Army Signalling Corps, and another was Arthur Shields (*see Fact 43*). By Tuesday morning, O'Kelly had managed to get a damaged 1.5 kilowatt ship's transmitter working again and David Bourke, an experienced Marconi operator, began to send out messages in Morse code:

> Irish Republic declared in Dublin today. Irish troops have
> captured city and are in full possession. Enemy cannot
> move in city. The whole country rising.

From then until the building had to be abandoned under
machine gun and sniper fire the next day, the message was
broadcast at regular intervals. In 1964 Marshall McLuhan
wrote: 'The Irish rebels used a ship's wireless to make, not
a point-to-point message, but a diffused broadcast in the
hope of getting word to some ship that would relay their
story to the American press.'[1]

This is widely accepted as the world's first radio
broadcast. The rebels, however, had no idea if their message
was being picked up, because they couldn't get any receiving
equipment to work.

But this Fact doesn't end there – while the story of the
first ever radio broadcast isn't very widely known, what's even
less widely known is that the rebels' broadcast was actually
intercepted, apparently by several receivers. From one ship
which did intercept the broadcast, however, there was no
chance of the rebel message being relayed to the American
press, because that ship was the British warship *HMS
Adventure*, anchored at Dun Laoghaire and being used as a
relay station for messages between Dublin and London.

In his book, *The Sea Hound*, Daire Brunicardi writes
that at 1.35 p.m. on Tuesday, the *Adventure's* radio operator

intercepted the first of three rebel messages. The next two were intercepted on Wednesday morning and included the somewhat slanted news that: 'British troops have been repulsed with great slaughter in the attempt to take the Irish position. The people are wildly enthusiastic for the new government.'

17

Receipts – official and unofficial politeness

The conduct of war in 1916 was a very different affair from the use of megadeath-dealing weapons we are unfortunately so familiar with today. That is not to say that a dead man's family felt any less traumatised in 1916 than they would today – it is simply to acknowledge that at times there was, paradoxically, a 'civilised' approach to warfare back then, before the invention of carpet bombing and thermonuclear devices.

Some of the paperwork that has survived from the Easter Rising shows that hastily written receipts, on what seem like scraps of paper, were issued by both sides for items taken and items returned. In one case, the 'items' consisted of 200 rebel prisoners!

On 6 May, at Broadstone railway station in Dublin, one Captain H.E. Chissy filled out a receipt which said:

> Received from Capt Branston
> 2/8 Notts and Derby Regt
> 200 (two hundred) Rebel prisoners
> Signed

HE Chissy [?] Capt
2/6 North Staff Regt
OC Escort

Two days later, on 8 May, Captain Branston was issued another receipt:

Received from Capt
HPG Branston 2/8
Sherwood Foresters,
100 (one hundred) pairs
of RIC handcuffs.
M Feeny
HC RIC

Apart from the recipient, the two receipts may be unrelated, but they could be interpreted as evidence that Captain Branston, having safely deposited the rebels at the railway station, took his time about returning the handcuffs used to 'secure' them!*

On the rebel side, meanwhile, receipts were issued for commandeered foodstuffs – in one instance, a receipt was left on the premises of Messrs Alex Findlater & Co, which said 'Commandeered by the Irish Republic, to be paid for, goods to the value of about £25. By Order of the IR Government.'

In another example, having secured the GPO on

Monday, some rebels went to the Metropole Hotel next door, where a Mr Oliver was manager. An eyewitness, L.G. Redmond-Howard, says that Mr Oliver 'all the while kept as cool as a cucumber' when a rebel officer 'arrayed in green and gold, wearing cocked hat and feathers and high top-boots, with a sword in one hand and a revolver in the other', arrived at the door, accompanied by two others 'each armed with a loaded rifle of modern pattern, with bayonets fixed.'

'We intend to commandeer your food supply,' said the man in the cocked hat, 'and I must ask you to show me the way to your provisions.'

For a second Mr Oliver hesitated. 'Suppose I refuse?' he said.

'In that case I will take them and you too,' was the reply, and then, addressing the two men, he added, 'Men, do your duty'.[1]

The men took what they came for, while Redmond-Howard wrote down a list of the goods. The officer then signed a receipt for the goods taken in the name of the Irish Republic and, added Redmond-Howard, 'Mr Oliver, much to my disappointment, pocketed the precious document'. The rebels then left, but were back minutes later – not to take more provisions, but to give the manager a £10 note.

I purchased the two receipts made out to Captain Branston from a seller in England in 2001. Among a large box of bric-a-brac the seller had bought in Nottingham was a picture in a tatty frame and, when he removed the frame, he discovered the receipts stuck to the back board. Unfortunately they were subsequently lost in the post between England and Ireland, so they're still out there somewhere!

18 Today's rebels – yesterday's Olympians

Bicycles featured largely as a means of transport during the rebellion – on the rebel side they were regularly used by dispatch riders and also as a means of 'hit and run' attacks on the British. But although they were faster than walking, bicycles weren't necessarily any safer; the first casualty claimed by the defenders of Trinity College was a young rebel dispatch rider (*see Fact 14*).

And not every proposed use of bicycles was approved – Margaret Skinnider, a rebel with the St Stephen's Green garrison which was under heavy fire from the Shelbourne Hotel, wanted to cycle past the hotel and lob in some bombs as she passed, but her commandant replied simply: 'too dangerous'.

Nevertheless, some success was had by a skirmishing patrol from the Jacob's factory garrison, who were sent out on bikes to relieve the pressure on de Valera's garrison in Boland's Mills – however, they paid a heavy price for that small success (*see Fact 14*).

An interesting fact about that bicycle patrol though, is that two of the rebel cyclists were no strangers to cycling

– the ironically-named Walker brothers, Michael and John, had both competed for Ireland on the Olympic cycling team in Stockholm in 1912 (Great Britain was permitted to have each 'home nation' compete separately and so teams from England, Scotland and Ireland entered). Their event was the 200-mile road race, which began at two in the morning! The Irish were the only team who not only had no spare bicycles, but didn't even have any spare wheels. As a team, they ranked eleventh, and individually, Mick finished sixty-eighth and John was in eighty-first place. Mick was also the 50-mile Irish champion and won several medals and cups for both the 50- and 100-mile events.

During the rebellion, Mick Walker also acted as a courier, and, being a familiar sight on his bicycle on the streets of Dublin, he successfully delivered many dispatches without challenge.

Following the surrender, both Mick and John managed to escape from Jacob's, but they were later arrested and sent to Stafford Detention Barracks. Mick's son, also Michael, said that his father was released when he was vouched for by a policeman who knew him from his cycling days with the Dublin Metropolitan Police (DMP). Most of the rebel detainees were eventually housed in a POW camp in Frongoch in Wales, and, since neither of the Walker brothers appear in the lists of Frongoch detainees (a John Walker is mentioned, but he is not Mick's brother), it seems likely that both Olympians were vouched for, having both cycled, and fought, for their country.

19

A crack shot in TCD

Communication between rebel positions was never easy during the rebellion, but in some parts of Dublin it was easier than others – at least, that is, while the phone lines were still intact. After the occupation of the GPO, an outpost was quickly set up directly across O'Connell Street in buildings on the corner of North Earl Street. Instructions and observations were exchanged between headquarters and the outpost for several days, until, inevitably, the phone line went dead.

The problem was solved when the commandant, W.J. Brennan-Whitmore, had the idea of setting up a communication 'cable', using a simple loop of twine anchored on either side of the street, with a tin canister attached to it. Messages would then be put into the canister and pulled across the street in safety. However, the Volunteers hadn't bargained on the shooting skills of some of the army snipers based on the roof of Trinity College. Shortly after the tin canister was put into service, it was pulled back into the outpost, displaying a new bullethole! It had been hit from a distance of some 500 metres – an impressive shot by any standard (Olympic competition distances are just 50 metres).

From then on, paper messages were instead tied directly to the twine – a system which was used successfully until the outpost was abandoned.

Coincidentally, after he'd been taken prisoner, Brennan-Whitmore met the man responsible for holing the canister: an Australian, probably on leave from the front, who had been drafted in to help with the defence of Trinity and who was a obviously a crack shot. When Brennan-Whitmore told him that the tin canister had been hit, the Aussie 'gave an exultant war-whoop and exclaimed: "Did I get it?"'[1]

20

What was life like for a rebel under fire?

A rebel Volunteer whose name doesn't appear in the official lists of deported prisoners, but who is included in the Roll of Honour, is Seosamh de Brún, who fought with B Company, 2nd Battalion, Dublin Brigade, in Jacob's factory.

In 1949, de Brún submitted a statement of his experiences to the Bureau of Military History – Witness Statement 312 – and in it he tells of his time with the rebels during the Easter Rising. However, this statement, written with hindsight, isn't the only memoir that de Brún left behind.

In 1916, de Brún, evidently a carpenter, kept a very small pocket diary ('Collins' Midget Diary'), which has survived to this day. At the start of 1916 his entries concern personal business – for example, his resolution to give up smoking and drinking until business improves and he clears some of his debt. However, the entries soon get more interesting – for instance, on Saturday, 22 January: 'Police raid on Countess M[arkievicz]. & others. Volunteers involved. Stood to arms all night.'

From then on, in between notes about unions, social visits and bank accounts, there are entries about munitions, Volunteer parades, printing press seizures and Volunteer expulsions. Fascinating as all that is, though, what sets this diary apart is that de Brún evidently carried it with him throughout the rebellion, making it possibly the only surviving diary written by a rank and file Volunteer 'under fire' (and therefore without the benefit of hindsight).

With tiny writing, on small pages, de Brún's diary isn't easy to decipher; nevertheless, unpublished as it is, the diary gives us a real flavour of what it was like to have been an ordinary Volunteer caught up in momentous events – events which weren't immediately popular with the local population. He notes: 'Populace don't understand … Tomorrow they will cheer us.'

Later he writes that he 'did not expect to be engaged in revolution … we expected the offensive would be forced on us.' He is content, however, with his predicament, saying: 'I review my life. I believe I was fated to be here today.'

Days passed in Jacob's without an attack, but with plenty of work to be done building barricades and performing guard duties. On Thursday, things were hotting up: 'Heavy firing … Suspense, tension. Darkness & silence save for the rattle of rifles & machine guns. Machine guns seem to be distinctive. Plug, plug, plug … sounds of bullets perforating walls. Expect to be riddled though inside building … can't sleep expecting attack which does not come.'

In fact, the British never did attack Jacob's, considering it easier and less costly (in terms of casualties) to bypass it. On Saturday, though, some of the Jacob's garrison took the fight to the enemy:

Called early & selected to form 'Diverting party'. De Valera at Westland Row hard pressed. 14 cyclists are ready. We proceed to … York St, St[ephen's] G[ree]n south, Leeson St towards Merrion Sq past Red Cross hospitals.

Soldiers at end of Sqr. Dismount opened fire remount return. Our fellows awful cool. Back same direction gauntlet of shots via York St. Snipers at top Grafton St.

O'Grady shot here. Helped along down York St past Col of Surgeons held by our fellows & back to factory.

He adds finally: 'I did not think I would return.' Volunteer O'Grady died shortly afterwards.

Interestingly, de Brún's diary ends on that Saturday, 29 April 1916, but inside the back cover a different hand continues the story and has written: 'This diary was found in Jacob's factory after the rising in Easter 1916. It was found by Edward Vaughan who was a fitter employed by the firm of Jacob's.' This is signed 'J. Doyle'. (The name J. Doyle is a mystery so far, but Edward Vaughan is recorded as having worked in the Engineering Department of Jacob's from 1913 until he retired in January 1954, at the age of sixty-five.)

The rebellion ended on Sunday, and in his official statement thirty-three years later, de Brún says that men wept bitterly with disappointment and many smashed their guns rather than surrender them. Then, in a probable explanation as to why his name doesn't appear on any prisoner lists, he adds: 'Numbers of the men were given the option to escape from the building and availed of it.' His first-hand account effectively ends there.

It's not unreasonable to conclude, therefore, that Seosamh de Brún was one of those who availed of the option to escape, and that, rather than be caught with such an incriminating document, he deliberately discarded his diary before leaving Jacob's.

21 What did Bella Glockler think?

History, as told by historians looking back, can be very dry, and when 'written by the winners' can be biased. Meanwhile, history as reported by contemporary writers and journalists, can be informative, but lifeless.

But history as told by ordinary people caught up in events can take us back in time, and we can find ourselves living the moment and feeling the emotions of the witness – even when we know, with hindsight, that an account was written with limited knowledge of greater events.

This is the reason why published diaries are so popular – we know we're getting an unedited version of the truth. Even though it's the truth as that single person saw it, incorporating their own slant, their own subjectivity, their own prejudices even, it is still a glimpse into a real, immediate window on the past and, with the luxury of hindsight, we can take an eyewitness account and relate it to our knowledge of the bigger picture. History can then really come to life.

In Fact 20 we had excerpts from the Easter Week diary of a rebel Volunteer under fire, but here are some excerpts from an unpublished diary of an ordinary civilian, Bella Glockler, caught up in the rebellion, worrying about her neighbours, herself and even her dog.

Unfortunately, other than what she wrote herself, we have no facts about who Bella was, where exactly she lived, nor even why she kept a diary during Easter week 1916. Yet from the pages of her diary, we can get some small insight into what kind of a person Bella was; we see the area she lived in and we can get a sense of the worries and fears that came from being caught up in the fighting, surrounded by streets under fire.

Bella's diary, as it comes down to us after more than ninety years, is a fragile typewritten document on very thin paper, most likely the carbon copy of the original, typed after the rebellion, but from notes written in the present tense. Perhaps she kept the copy for herself and mailed the original to a friend or relation (or vice versa!).

It runs to six pages, starting on Easter Monday, 24 April, and ending sixteen days later on Wednesday, 10 May – from 'This afternoon an army of Sinn Feiners took possession of most of the big buildings including the GPO', to 'The milkman turned up after ten days: he was held a prisoner for two days near Church Street by the S. Feiners.'

Bella doesn't give us the name of her own street, but from the streets she does mention, we know she was living in a 'hot' zone, near O'Connell Street. Indeed on Tuesday she writes: 'machine guns were firing up and down Killarney Street, Gloucester [now Seán McDermott] Street and Seville Place.' On Wednesday: 'There is a big gun on top of Amiens Street Station … which fires straight up Talbot Street …', and 'A tenement house up Buckingham Street, half a minute walk from here was shelled nearly all day.'

Bella also tells us about the effects that a sudden rebellion could have on ordinary life: 'We can't go out and get food … It is impossible to settle down to do anything as the shots are terrifying … The gas has been turned off since Monday night. People have been risking their lives all day to get food … Went with a neighbour … to try to get bread. I was told I would have to fight to get it.'

She mentions sympathetically that a neighbour who was accidentally shot dead had 'escaped the *Lusitania* disaster last year'. Elsewhere she notes that: 'the poor dog is nearly out of her mind'. After the ceasefire, she sees the ruins of the city centre: 'It goes to one's heart to see the desolation.' But Bella's sympathy has its limits – when she hears about looters, she writes: 'All the riff-raff have turned out …'

There is more information to be had from Bella's six short pages, but there are also questions raised that we may never answer. Her name, for instance, is an unusual one for Dublin of 1916. Was she even Irish? Is there a clue in the fact that she twice mentions trying to get to the American Consulate? The Consulate was on Merrion Square in 1916 and Bella 'was escorted by a sentry with fixed bayonet', only to find that the Consul wasn't there.

With further research, more will be learned about Bella Glockler, but for now we can simply be grateful that she took the time to leave us her own unique view of the Easter Rising and its effect on an ordinary person – a viewpoint that, until now, has probably been unknown for over ninety years.

22 Duelling snipers

As in all urban warfare, snipers featured largely in the tactics of both sides throughout the rebellion. Acting alone and highly mobile, with the ability to fire and disappear, snipers can have a devastating effect on their enemy – not just by killing or wounding, but arguably more so by undermining morale. A single sniper can pin down a large number of opponents, simply by making them afraid to move from safety.

Lethally clever tactics are often used by snipers – on one occasion, British soldiers telephoned a shop which was known to be occupied by rebels and military snipers waited to shoot whoever moved into view to pick up the receiver, which was by a window. As it happened, a rebel captain went to answer the call, but was tackled to the ground by a quick-thinking comrade.

Nevertheless, rebel snipers, it could be said, had the upper hand for two reasons – firstly, they would have had local knowledge of rooftops and other vantage points. Secondly, since the majority didn't wear a uniform, as soon as they put their weapon out of sight, they 'became' a civilian. (It has been said, though, that the British sometimes examined the shoulders of suspected men to see if they were bruised from the massive recoil of the Howth Mauser – *see Fact 5*).

This civilian 'camouflage', combined with increasing casualties and decreasing morale, had a terrible effect on the military, with the result that, unable to tell rebel from civilian, non-combatants often became innocent victims. One witness wrote that snipers 'seemed to be everywhere, but it was almost impossible to locate them. Troops … were picked off from windows and roofs … in the most bewildering fashion … till the military were tempted to fire on any strange figure looming up in the distance.'[1]

However, there are several recorded instances of British snipers themselves adopting the urban camouflage of the civilian. At one point in the fighting around St Stephen's Green, a British sniper dressed himself as a maid and set to his task from a window in the Shelbourne Hotel. For some time, his disguise was successful, although eventually he was discovered and eliminated.

In the South Dublin Union, Volunteer Robert Holland noticed an increase in the accuracy of enemy sniping and at the same time saw a woman leaning out of a window in a house opposite his post. Acting on a hunch and thinking that 'it was a queer place for a woman to be and that it was queer she should have a hat on her, as she must have seen the bullets flying around … I made up my mind … I fired at her. She sagged half way out of the window. The hat … fell off her and I saw what I took to be a woman was a man in his shirt sleeves.'[2]

Meanwhile his post comrade, Mick Liston, was proving to be a formidable sniper for the rebels, with more than a dozen confirmed hits, including one 200-yard shot which left a British sniper dangling from a tree for a day.

There were sniper 'heroes' on the British side as well – a number of sharpshooters operated from the Bermingham Tower in Dublin Castle, firing on rebels in Jacob's factory and the Four Courts across the Liffey. The tower was draped in large sheets of canvas to provide cover for the snipers, one of whom, by Thursday, was credited with more than twenty hits.

Unfortunately though, some rebel snipers continued their activity past the official ceasefire (*see Fact 31*).

23 Ruling the waves

The sea – with its coastline, its ports and as a means of transport – barely featured in the rebel leaders' plans for the Easter Rising, apart from the attempted, but doomed, landing of an arms shipment in Kerry (*see Fact 2*).

However, with its tradition of 'ruling the waves' the British Navy was ready and able to respond to rebel activity around the coast of Ireland – often with great success. From a gunboat in Dublin's Liffey basin (*see Fact 37*) to a warship in Galway Bay (*see Fact 13*) and the interception of rebel broadcasts (*see Fact 16*), the British Navy played a much larger part in suppressing the rebellion than many might have realised.

The larger engagements are dealt with elsewhere in this book, but some of the minor engagements are worth mentioning.

On Thursday, 27 April, a contingent of Royal Munster Fusiliers were landed for the defence of Galway, followed by more troops from the cruiser *HMS Gloucester*. The *Gloucester* was later used in the transfer of prisoners taken in Galway.

In Cork, the battleship *HMS Albemarle* anchored at Passage West and, although not called into action, her four 12-inch guns and complement of 2,000 marines served as a very effective 'floating threat', with rumours doing the rounds that she was there to bombard Cork city. Some of her marines were landed to garrison the naval base on Haulbowline Island which, overnight, was 'lined with tents, gun emplacements, light guns [and] machine guns'. (One foggy night during this operation, a sentry challenged a moving figure and, getting no answer, fired into the darkness, hitting his target in the head. On examination, however, the victim turned out to be a donkey and an expensive donkey at that – Admiral Sir Lewis Bayly remarked that: 'It cost me two pounds: one pound to the sentry for having made such a good shot and one pound to the old woman who owned the animal.'[1])

In Kerry, two platoons of marines with two machine guns were landed in Fenit from the *HMS Primrose* to protect its naval base, while the *HMS Iris* deposited one platoon and one machine gun at Sybil Head to defend the signal station – a post which was attacked by rebels on 1 May, with three British casualties (*see Fact 48*).

Closer to Dublin, on Wednesday, the armed yacht *Boadicea II* was ordered to Skerries, following information received that the town's Wireless Telegraph station was in imminent danger of attack. Although the number of rebels reported to be on the march was wildly exaggerated, it seems that the area Commandant, Thomas Ashe, had plans to attack the station, but changed his mind on seeing the *Boadicea II* in the harbour. Later on, the *HMS Dee* transported 170 troops to Skerries, thus ending any threat of rebel assault.

Meanwhile, Arklow's defence against a potential advance of rebels from Enniscorthy to Dublin was boosted by the presence of two armed trawlers.

There are other instances of Britain using its navy to good advantage during the rebellion, but suffice to say that the sea was one theatre of operations where they enjoyed complete supremacy over the rebels.

24 Boy soldiers

The youngest participant in the rebellion was probably twelve-year-old Tommy Keenan, who marched with the Irish Citizen Army at the start of the rebellion on Monday. However, having been ordered home to tell his parents what he was up to, young Keenan found himself locked in his room by his father, who obviously feared for his son's safety.

Nevertheless, Tuesday soon found young Keenan back with the Citizen Army in the College of Surgeons – in defiance of his father, he had climbed out of a window and shimmied down a drainpipe to rejoin the garrison.

Meanwhile, author James Stephens wrote in his account of the Rising that: 'Among these [rebels in St Stephen's Green] were some who were only infants – one boy seemed about 12 years of age. He was strutting the centre of the road with a large revolver in his small fist.' In the same commentary, Stephens added: 'Small boys do not believe that people will really kill them, but small boys were killed.'[1]

Unfortunately this proved terribly true, for while Tommy Keenan probably had the adventure of a lifetime, the *Sinn Féin Rebellion Handbook* lists at least four twelve-year-olds among the civilian dead interred in Glasnevin. Indeed, some victims were younger than twelve – among them was one J.F. Foster, aged two years and ten months.[2]

Opposing the rebels, possibly the youngest participant was one Private Neville Nicholas Fryday of the 75th Battalion Canadian Infantry. Although born in Thurles, Private Fryday was in a Canadian uniform when he was caught up in the rebellion – his parents were William and Elizabeth A. Fryday, of Mill House, Shankill, County Dublin, and he was possibly on leave, visiting them.

Young Private Fryday died of wounds on Sunday, 30 April 1916, and is buried in Dublin's Mount Jerome Cemetery. In the *Rebellion Handbook*, his age is poignantly given as '16 and a half' and his address as 'Mercer's Hospital'.

Fact 1: One of the houses destroyed by the German bombardment of Lowestoft on Tuesday morning.
All photographs are author's collection unless otherwise stated.

Fact 2: The German gun-runner, the *Aud*, which ended its voyage at the bottom of the sea.

Fact 5: A British soldier examines some of the Howth Mausers.

Fact 6: Some of the pikes carried by the rebels are collected together.

ERECTED
BY HIS SORROWING WIDOW
IN LOVING MEMORY OF
HER DEAR HUSBAND
CHARLES HAYTER
WHO WAS ACCIDENTALLY SHOT
8TH APRIL 1916
IN HIS 75TH YEAR

140229 PRIVATE
N. N. FRYDAY
75TH BN. CANADIAN INF.
30TH APRIL 1916

AND HIS SISTER
MARTHA(MELA RICHARDSON
17TH APRIL 1965.
"AT PEACE"

Fact 10: The grave of Charles Hayter (above), a grocer killed during the fighting in the Mount Street Bridge area. Interestingly, he lies between Private Neville Fryday (right; *see fact 24*) and Rifleman D. Wilson killed on Easter Monday.

Fact 11: The burned remains of The O'Rahilly's De Dion Bouton car, used as part of a barricade during the Rising.

Fact 12: A view of the Shelbourne Hotel from the direction of the Royal College of Surgeons. It's obvious that the rebels in St Stephen's Green were at the mercy of British gunfire.

Fact 14: Although not quite the kind of bicycle used by rebels during the Rising, this is an interesting photo of Michael, John and Richard Walker (*see fact 18*) riding a trandem past the ruined GPO. *Courtesy Derek Jones.*

Fact 15: Volunteer Mick Edwards who, along with brother John, fought in the rebellion and was detained in Frongoch internment camp.

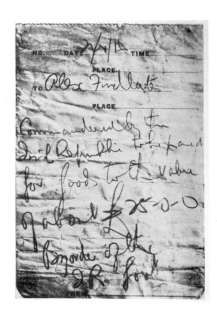

Fact 17:
Examples of
the receipts
issued by both
sides during the
rebellion.

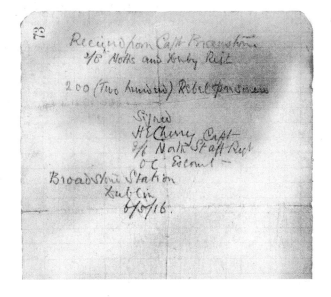

Fact 21: Soldiers distributing bread because of food shortages experienced during the Rising.

Fact 22: British soldiers taking cover from a sniper.

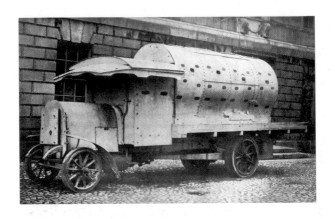

Fact 27: Examples of both types of armoured lorry which were produced at speed to ensure the safe movement of men and equipment through the streets of Dublin.

Fact 25: O'Connell Street ruined. When Bella Glockler saw all that was left of the city centre, she wrote: 'It goes to one's heart to see the desolation.'

Fact 28: A contemporary postcard showing the 'Royal Naval Mobile Gun Detachment, Sinn Fein Rebellion, Ireland 1916'. It's not known where the photo was taken, or who precisely the men are, but it's possible they are the men who operated the naval artillery piece which was mounted on a lorry for use against the rebels. *Courtesy Nick Goad.*

Fact 29: A Volunteer in uniform.

Fact 32: A soldier tends the temporary resting place of Private Arthur Charles Smith, who died on the Saturday of Easter week. The exact location of his burial is still marked by a plaque along the Nassau Street side of TCD.

Fact 33: Trinity College's main gate is guarded against rebels, but students were allowed through to sit exams!

Fact 37: The *Helga*, which shelled the rebels during 1916, but later became the Irish patrol vessel, the *Muirchu*.

Fact 38: The Royal College of Surgeons. The damage caused by bullets fired from the direction of the Shelbourne Hotel is clearly visible.

FIELD SERVICE
POCKET BOOK
1914.

Fact 40: Captain A.A. Dickson's Field Service Pocket Book still bears the scar of a rebel bullet. *Courtesy Imperial War Museum.*

Fact 41: Captain Arthur Annan Dickson, who commanded one of the firing squads which dealt the ultimate punishment to the rebel leaders.
Courtesy John McGuiggan.

Fact 44: Major John Lowe, seen beside his father Brigadier General W.H.M. Lowe, accepting P.H. Pearse's unconditional surrender.

From Commander of Dublin Forces
To P. H. Pearce

29. April/16
1.40 P.M.

A woman has come in and tells me you wish to negotiate with me. I am prepared to receive you in BRITAIN ST at the North End of MOORE ST provided that you surrender unconditionally. You will proceed up MOORE ST accompanied only by the woman who brings you this note under a white flag —

W. N. Lowe
B. Genl.

Fact 44: Brigadier General Lowe's communication to Pearse, dictated to his son, Major Lowe, in which the major misspelled Pearse's name.

Fact 45: A clock in the GPO, surrounded by evidence of the destruction caused by the rebellion.

Fact 46: Men of the Dublin Corporation Fire Brigade at one of the city's many destroyed buildings.

Fact 47: One of the silver cups awarded to the defenders of TCD. This example was awarded to Cadet E.R. Murray, who helped bring Private Smith into the college grounds from where he lay wounded on Nassau Street.

Fact 49: One of the souvenir booklets on sale very quickly after the end of the Rising.

Fact 50: The interior of the GPO was completely destroyed by the British bombardment – however, they could pour their shells into the building, but they couldn't stop the rebels from singing!

25 Foreign fighters

Arrayed against the Irish rebels were soldiers from many nations, but all with Commonwealth and Empire in common – as well as the English, Scots and Welsh, there were Australians, New Zealanders, South Africans and Canadians.

But the international composition of the combatants wasn't confined to the British side – the rebels were joined by a small number of non-Irish fighters during the course of the Rising, although pinning down their precise nationalities is not an easy task!

According to an issue of *An t-Óglach*, the army journal, from 23 January 1926, among the reinforcements who trickled into the GPO on the first day of the Rising were 'two seafaring men – a Finn and a Swede – who did not know very much English. Under cross-examination they explained with difficulty but obvious earnestness that "they … didn't like England" … They were given rifles and actually fought on the roof of the GPO.'

An account in Max Caulfield's *The Easter Rebellion* mentions what must be the same pair of sailors, but identifies them as a Finn and a Pole, who explained that being from small nations they wanted to fight on the side of a small nation – and also that they understood guns. 'Tell them they're welcome', was James Connolly's reply to their request.

However, another source refers to them as 'a pair of Swedish sailors who … were prepared to fight until Thursday, when their ship was scheduled to leave.' (Unfortunately, however, just after being armed with two shotguns, one sailor's weapon went off and badly wounded a Volunteer.)

This confusion over nationality wasn't restricted to the rebels, though – in the official lists of detainees, one 'Makanaltis, Antli (Russian), Belfast – Seaman' is listed among 308 prisoners removed from Richmond Barracks, Dublin, on 2 May and lodged in Knutsford Detention Barracks on 3 May. Then, on 29 May, 'the military authorities, having fully investigated' their cases, the release of 238 men was ordered, including one 'Makipaltis, Antle Zecks, Finland' – surely the same man and perhaps even one of the GPO's defenders who decided to stay on and missed his boat's departure.

Meanwhile, a Spaniard somehow managed to get involved in the fighting as well and his total lack of English caused a problem when he needed to be treated by a medic. Eventually a priest, speaking part church Latin and part simple Spanish, managed to communicate with him.

There was also at least one American fighting with the rebels. He fought in the GPO, an unnamed revolutionary who addressed others as 'comrade' and was fatally wounded during the evacuation when a bullet hit a haversack of ammunition he was carrying, causing him to lose a huge volume of blood.

Finally, among the thousands of names, ranks, professions and even addresses meticulously recorded in the *Sinn Féin Rebellion Handbook*, there's a passing mention of some 'Indian students from the King's Inns, who performed ambulance work', but who apparently didn't warrant having their names recorded for posterity.

26 Small memories, big impact

One of the fascinating things about diaries is that no matter how many survive to give descriptions of the same event, each one is still unique, giving its own impressions and its own viewpoint of that event.

Excerpts from Easter Week diaries are mentioned in some of these 50 facts, but, of course, not many witnesses left full diaries – sometimes all that comes down to us from 1916 are snippets, short memories of single events, often not even written down, but mentioned whenever the subject of Ireland's rebellion is talked about, and inevitably followed with 'I must write that down some day ...'

Of course, it is usually assumed that 'small' memories, personal events that don't bear mentioning in the histories, aren't important, but these are the memories that help bring history back to the personal level. Our own memories are fragile things to begin with, and 'handed down' memories are even more easily forgotten. And even when we get a chance to re-tell those handed down tales, it's inevitable that, despite all our good intentions, details get blurred in the telling.

However, the simplest way of securing a memory is to just write it down, so if you have a memory of your own, or a tale you were told by a parent or grandparent, do your best to put it on paper as soon as you can.

In that spirit, here are some examples of 'small' memories, none of which are necessarily historically important, but all of which add to our understanding of history as a human event. Some of them have been published, in some cases privately, but others are handed down memories, finally committed to paper.

Ingrid MacDermot was eighteen months old in 1916, living on Dublin's Fitzwilliam Square. On Easter Monday, her parents were enjoying the Bank Holiday at the races in Fairyhouse, where a horse called *All Sorts* won the Grand National (the interestingly-named *Civil War* only came third, but won in 1914!). Ingrid was at home in the care of her nanny, yet when her parents got back to Dublin, the baby was gone – Ingrid's nanny had disobeyed instructions by leaving the house, taking the baby and going to visit her army boyfriend in barracks on the north side of the city. Meanwhile the rebellion had begun, and nanny and baby couldn't get back across the city. Fortunately, after some frantic searching, Ingrid was reunited with her parents, so the story had a happy ending – for the MacDermots at least, since we don't know what punishment was meted out to the nanny.

In the 1960s, a Mrs Daly was a voluntary worker with An Taisce, the National Trust for Ireland, and on rare occasions she spoke of her memories of a time when she did some administrative work for General Sir John Maxwell, the British Commander-in-Chief in 1916. Working through some army lists, she noticed that a particular pair of initials appeared alongside a surprising number of men's names. Turning to Maxwell she said that she knew about military awards like the DCM, MC, and even VC, but what, she wondered, was the VD and how did so many men have it? Maxwell, not particularly remembered for his diplomacy, told Miss Daly to ask her mother when she got home. (Interestingly, Mrs Daly's father had been in Dun Laoghaire when the British reinforcements landed, and was approached by an officer who spoke to him in French – *see Fact 9*.)

In another Easter Monday tale, an early memory of Louise Hutton's was seeing a group of men near St Stephen's Green, carrying shovels and pick-axes – an unusual enough sight on a Bank Holiday that they even made a memorable impression on a four-year-old. As it turned out, of course, the men weren't workers, but members of the Irish Citizen Army, about to entrench themselves in the Green for a short time before been driven out by machine gun fire from the Shelbourne Hotel (*see Fact 12*).

Meanwhile, on the Wednesday, Lieutenant John

Samuel Carrothers noted in a letter home from Ship Street Barracks that: 'The Sinn Feiners are rotten shots … A chap was standing in the open street and they fired a volley at him but never hit him.' Later in the same letter he remarks that: 'It is wonderful how soon one gets used to fighting. We lounge about here reading and yawning while volleys are being fired over our heads. It is very boring listening to crack of rifles all day.'

However, firing over your head is one thing, but it is another thing entirely to have your car 'riddled with bullets' while driving along the quays in Dublin, which is just what happened to Lord Dunsany. Nevertheless, it wasn't that incident which became one of Dunsany's strongest memories of the rebellion, nor was it the 'hole in my face' that he got from rebel gunfire minutes later. Instead it was a remark made by a nun in Jervis Street Hospital, 'in the thick of the fighting', where he was being treated. Sister M. Basil 'looked out of the window where [bullets] were cracking by, and said of them: "the nasty little things". This lofty disdain would have been appropriate to flies that were teasing a patient, but I had not before heard man or woman speak quite in that way of bullets.'

27
Delivering soldiers instead of stout

In June 1916, German soldiers at the front in France were astonished to be confronted by Britain's latest military invention – it was then that the tank lumbered and clanked its way into history. Back in Ireland, however, 'tanks' of another sort were seen on the streets of Dublin during the rebellion in April.

On Wednesday, Volunteers in the GPO watched in amazement as a fully-armoured lorry rumbled down O'Connell Street towards them. It was one of probably five such vehicles that were constructed in haste the day before. The brainwave of Colonel B.P. Portal, commander of the Curragh mobile column, the actual design is attributed to Colonel H.T.W. Allatt. 'Most ingenious conveyances', according to one commentator.[1]

The raw materials for the armoured 'cars' consisted of Daimler lorries borrowed from the Guinness brewery, as well as a number of locomotive boilers and a quantity of steel plate. Two different designs were built – one was made from four boilers placed together to form a single curved, enclosed space (and looking 'like a cross between a submarine and a baker's van'[2]), and the other was a more straightforward arrangement of flat steel plates, forming a box-like structure.

Slits were made in the armour surrounding the cab for drivers to peer through, while loopholes were cut into the sides, both for air to come in and for soldiers to fire out of (dummy holes were also painted alongside to confuse the enemy). Accommodating as many as twenty-two troops, according to one account, the interior of both designs must have been extremely uncomfortable: 'The noise of the rifles in such a confined space was stupendous.'[3]

At least it was safer inside than out on the open streets. One soldier described the experience of being driven through a hot zone: 'Every bullet clanged and jarred through your head.'[4] And in some cases, it may have been more than just the bullet's noise that jarred through the head …

One of the Volunteers watching the crude machine from the GPO that Wednesday was Joseph Sweeney and while his comrades' bullets were having little impact on the lorry, Sweeney aimed carefully for the driver's slit. His first few shots had no effect, but then one seemed to hit home, because the vehicle halted and the engine went dead. The lorry stayed exactly where it was halted for some time, until another armoured Daimler arrived to tow it away.

Mainly, however, it seems the armoured lorries were

used as a secure means of transport, for both soldiers and equipment. In one assault on the Four Courts garrison, an armoured lorry safely deposited sixteen sharpshooters to a churchyard on the opposite side of the River Liffey, from where they fired at the rebels from behind tombstones. The lorry then returned towing an artillery piece, which was used to shell the rebel position.

Along Capel Street and North King Street the fighting was particularly intense, and the lorries were used to help in a slow grinding down of the rebel forces. Typically, the contraption was backed up to a target building, with a machine gun laying down suppressing fire if necessary. A party of troops carrying crowbars and axes would then jump out and secure the building. The lorry would return to British lines and the process would be repeated. Progress was made, but it was frustratingly slow – at one point, the British took fourteen hours to advance less than 650 metres. However, slow though it may have been, progress was nevertheless made and the improvised armoured vehicles played an important part in the success of the British forces' defeat of the rebels.

After the rebellion had 'officially' ended, but the danger of sniping was still real, one of the square-sided armoured Daimlers was used in the delivery of cash to post offices around the city for the payment of the separation allowance to families of soldiers on active duty. More then £10,000 in silver was collected from the Bank of Ireland and delivered 'in perfect safety'.[5]

Eventually though, the Daimler lorries had their armour removed and they went back to Guinness to resume their quiet job of delivering stout instead of soldiers. Colonel Allatt, meanwhile, became a casualty of the Rising, having been fatally wounded in the South Dublin Union area, but was later mentioned in dispatches for distinguished services.

28 Mobile marine artillery

During the Rising, the British naval vessel, *HMS Adventure*, was in Dublin Bay, operating as a relay station for messages between Dublin and London (*see Fact 16*). But this wasn't the only role her crew played during the rebellion.

Given the urgent need for artillery to help subdue the rebels in Dublin, a six-pounder from an armed trawler was landed on-shore, and *Adventure's* gunnery lieutenant and several artificers worked through Wednesday night to mount the weapon on a horse-drawn coal lorry and armour it with steel plate. At 8 a.m. on Thursday morning, two naval gun crews started off towards the city, with ammunition being carried in a hand cart.

The gun and its crew made their way to Mount Street Bridge, and it was sited in Percy Place. By the time it was made ready, however, the Battle of Mount Street Bridge (*see Fact 39*) was over, so instead it was directed against a new target.

Daire Brunicardi's *The Sea Hound* quotes a report by Captain Alpin (in charge at Dun Laoghaire) which states that the hastily prepared gun was used in action against 'Boland's

Mill, etc' – this was Éamon de Valera's rebel headquarters. Meanwhile Max Caulfield's *The Easter Rebellion* says that the gun in action against Boland's was a one-pounder taken from the *Helga* and mounted on a lorry. However, the chances of there being two jury-rigged, lorry-mounted, naval artillery pieces in use against the same building are pretty slim, so in all likelihood, there was only one.

In any case, by Friday, *Adventure* received word that the gun had fired 88 rounds on Thursday and was 'still going strong'.[1]

From Percy Place, the gun was taken by two battalions of the Sherwood Foresters, as they proceeded towards the Royal Hospital Kilmainham, to be used against any rebel-held houses encountered along the way. Unfortunately it is not known where the gun ended its rebellion service, or whether it made its way back on board ship.

Meanwhile, the *Sinn Féin Rebellion Handbook* lists a number of naval servicemen among the wounded – two Royal Marines and one Mercantile Marine fireman.

The *Handbook* also lists one Royal Navy fatality, although in fact he wasn't a victim of rebel action. Engine Room Artificer Robert Glaister was shot dead at the Northern Hotel on Amiens Street by Private Henry Wyatt of the 6th Royal Lancers. Wyatt was subsequently charged with murder, but found guilty of manslaughter and sentenced to five years' penal servitude.

29 Brothers in arms II

In Fact 15, we saw that many rebels fought side by side with their brothers, fathers or sons. However, it is also a fact that many families found themselves on opposite sides of the insurrection.

Conscription was not in force in Ireland, but soldiering in the British army was nevertheless a deliberately chosen profession for some Irishmen, especially those loyal to the Empire. However, for many poor Irishmen, it was simply a means of providing for their families, since their wives, the so-called 'separation women' (or 'shawlies'), received an allowance while their husbands were in uniform.

As it happened, many of those Irish recruits had brothers who, poor or not, couldn't bring themselves to join the British army and instead went in the entirely opposite direction, bearing arms against the British during the rebellion. And the interesting fact is that, during the rebellion, many of these khaki-clad Irishmen came face-to-face with their rebel brothers.

For example, on Tuesday, during the fierce fighting which marked the attack by the British on the rebel-held offices of the *Mail & Express*, opposite the gates of Dublin Castle, a soldier of the Dublin Fusiliers came face-to-face with a rebel who happened to be his younger brother. 'Run, you young fool, run!' he demanded, lowering his bayonet so his brother could make a getaway.[1]

Later in the week, one Volunteer recalled, as he and his comrades were being processed after surrendering, officers went among them taking names – one officer, however, just looked at a particular rebel and, without saying anything, wrote down his name and continued on.

'Does that officer know you?' the rebel was asked.

'That's my brother,' was the reply.[2]

In another incident during the rebel surrender, Volunteer Seosamh de Brún (*see Fact 20*) recalled that as Jacob's factory was being taken over by a detachment of the Dublin Fusiliers: 'by a curious coincidence as one brother left the factory in the Republican ranks another marched into it in the uniform of the British army'.

Of course, it also happened that some Irishmen in British uniform decided that they couldn't fight against their countrymen, and decided to fight with them instead – for example, also in Jacob's was Joe Byrne, home on leave from the Western Front, who, on the spur of the moment, had decided to join the rebels. In another example, the prisoner lists in the *Sinn Féin Rebellion Handbook* include a T. Parker, whose occupation is listed as 'Private with the 2nd Leinster Regiment'.

30 Skeffy's companions in death

The tragic story of how Francis Sheehy-Skeffington (Skeffy), an innocent non-combatant who was in fact opposed to the rebellion, was illegally executed by a criminally insane British officer during the week of the insurrection is possibly one of the better-known events of the Easter Rising.

In fact, three men were illegally executed in barracks in Rathmines on the orders of one Captain J.C. Bowen-Colthurst. Having ordered their detention on Tuesday, Bowen-Colthurst spent all night considering the situation and, finally deciding that the three prisoners were 'dangerous characters',[1] took it upon himself to have them marched into a yard on Wednesday morning and summarily shot. A Royal Commission of Inquiry later found Bowen-Colthurst guilty but insane and he was sent to Broadmoor Criminal Asylum, where he served less than two years of his sentence.

Some accounts of this incident don't even mention, let alone name, the two other men who died alongside Sheehy-Skeffington, while other accounts do, but give little other detail – in 1916, Skeffy was a very familiar face on the streets of Dublin and his murder alone was a big enough news story that it left the other deaths somewhat in the shade.

However, apart from Sheehy-Skeffington, Bowen-Colthurst was actually responsible for four other deaths. One was nineteen-year-old James Joseph Coade, who he shot in the head outside Rathmines Catholic church. Another was Volunteer Richard O'Carroll, a Dublin city councillor, who, after questioning, was shot in the back by Bowen-Colthurst. When told by a soldier that the writhing O'Carroll wasn't dead yet, the officer said: 'Never mind, he'll die later. Take him into the street', whereupon the Volunteer was dragged outside and left in a gutter.[2]

Facing the firing squad along with Sheehy-Skeffington, were two other men who were just as innocent as their more famous companion. Thomas Dickson and Patrick MacIntyre were both newspaper editors and, politically, were loyalists who opposed the Rising.

Elsie Mahaffy, daughter of the Provost of TCD, wrote in her diary that these two victims were 'ruffians, editors of sedition and indecent papers', although she doesn't explain her reasons, and it should be noted that she also wrote that Bowen-Colthurst was 'one of the best young men I have ever met'.[3]

Patrick MacIntyre, aged thirty-eight and described as

'medium height and burly', was editor of *The Searchlight*. Thomas Dickson, 'a Scotch-man' aged thirty-one and described as 'tiny ... about four feet six, a grotesque figure in a black coat and with curious eyes',[4] was editor of *The Eye-Opener*, which, according to the *Sinn Féin Rebellion Handbook* was 'a small paper, which had a short but sensational career, terminating with Dickson's death'. The *Handbook* adds intriguingly that: 'during Dickson's business career some of his undertakings had involved himself and other persons in very unfortunate circumstances'.

In fact, *The Eye-Opener* was a paper which reported on topics that passed for scandal and gossip in those more innocent days. In its issue dated 22 April, just four days before Dickson was shot, there are articles on 'Men who Lead Double Lives', 'Married Man and Two Girls' and even 'Bogus Dentists'. There are also several letters from correspondents threatening to reveal the names of those involved in 'the vices prevailing in this city', such as 'a certain married man ... on very intimate terms with a girl typist', and 'a young lady manageress of a leading tea rooms monopolising the time of a married man ...'

Interestingly, much of that final edition's editorial is concerned with its continued publication 'in spite of all the obstacles that have been or may be placed in our way'. With its mission of 'cleansing our city of some of the pests and evils that infest it', *The Eye-Opener* claimed that it had therefore 'brought down upon our heads the wrath of many highly placed individuals … Desperate measures are being adopted by them for the purpose of ending the production of *The Eye-Opener*.'

Fortunately for its detractors, the illegal execution of its editor was one obstacle that the paper couldn't survive – the 22 April issue was the last one ever published.

31 Deadly rooftops

We've seen that snipers were a major feature of the Rising, with terrible casualties inflicted on both sides during the week of the rebellion. However, an unfortunate fact is that a number of rebel snipers continued their deadly activities after the rebel headquarters and outposts had surrendered on Saturday and Sunday. According to an eyewitness: 'It was dastardly fighting, if it could be called fighting at all.'[1]

Almost by definition, snipers work alone and often on their own initiative, so it is possible that some of them simply hadn't heard the news of the surrender. It is also possible, of course, that some of them were deliberately flaunting the ceasefire and continuing their own personal war against the British – we'll never know.

According to one contemporary writer: 'Although the military gave the order to cease fire on Saturday afternoon, the streets of Dublin did not become quite safe for a couple of days following, because individual snipers who did not get word of the surrender, and some of them who did, but who preferred to meet death where they were, held on grimly to their positions.'[2]

Whatever the individual reasons, the fact is that, as author St John G. Ervine wrote: 'The rebellion was virtually over on the Saturday following Easter Monday, but for the best part of the succeeding week there was still some difficult work to be done in rounding up the snipers who had taken to the roofs of houses. In places like Merrion Square they were virtually immune from discovery. They could run along the roofs, hidden by parapets, and fire on the troops with the minimum chance of detection; but their position was a hopeless one. Death or discovery was inevitable, and in a few days the last of the snipers was taken.'

However, while the last of the snipers may have been silenced, the unfortunate possibility was that even when it was death that silenced them, discovery wasn't always inevitable – a special proclamation was issued by the civic authorities on Wednesday 3 May:

> The removal of bodies in Dublin is being carried out by the military authorities and the sanitary authorities, and citizens are required to give information of discoveries of bodies to the police, or to the Medical Officer of Health, Castle Street. Bodies may yet be lying on roofs or concealed in chimneys, from which snipers fired.

32 Bodies buried and bodies burned

Desperate times call, of course, for desperate measures and in the heat of a warm week in spring, the condition of dead bodies left in the open air became desperate fairly quickly. With safe removal and interment impossible under the circumstances, the temporary burial of the rebellion's casualties became an urgent necessity and many of the deceased were therefore buried as near as practicable to where they fell.

In Trinity College, three casualties were buried within the grounds – two soldiers and a rebel. The rebel had been shot dead while cycling past the college and his body brought into the provost's house (*see Fact 14*). Elsie Mahaffy, the college provost's daughter, wrote in her diary that he had a rifle and a revolver, as well as plenty of ammunition and money. She added:

> For three days he lay in College, in an empty room. When necessary he was buried in the Park and later when quiet was restored was disinterred and sent to the morgue, but during the fortnight while he lay in College, though well

dressed and from a respectable street, no one ever came to ask for his body.[1]

In the area of the Battle of Mount Street Bridge, seven temporary interments were made. Three soldiers were buried in the grounds of St Bartholomew's church on Clyde Road, while two others were buried in the rear of the parochial hall on Northumberland Road. However, despite the continued efforts of the Town Clerk of Pembroke Urban District Council, Joshua C. Manly, their bodies weren't disinterred until 12 May, nearly two weeks after the Rising ended.

Manly had more success organising the early disinterment of non-military victims: Volunteer Lieutenant Michael Malone, who was buried in uniform in the front garden of 25 Northumberland Road, and a civilian buried at the parochial hall, also on Northumberland Road. These were removed on 9 and 10 May by the Guardians of the Poor.

Meanwhile, in Dublin Castle, a voluntary nurse wrote that the windows where she worked overlooked the Castle garden, 'where all day about twenty men were digging graves. The nearest were for officers, each made separately; then two large graves for Tommies and civilians, and, far away by themselves, the Sinn Féiners. ... Most of [the bodies] were removed when the rebellion was over ...'[2]

Even when removal of remains was no longer dangerous, the number of deceased became a problem in some cases, and the solution was to have a mass burial – in St Paul's cemetery, near the main cemetery in Glasnevin, there is a mass grave for 1916 victims.

In other cases, of course, interment of victims wasn't a possibility, since the buildings they died in were consumed by fire. At Mount Street Bridge, Clanwilliam House burned so comprehensively that, although three rebels died there, when it was searched for remains 'not a particle of flesh or bone was found' apart from one human leg, which was subsequently buried 'in a proper Christian manner'.[3] One witness remarked on the lingering 'smell of roasting flesh'.[4]

33 Testing times indeed

For some people, a school or college exam is a very stressful thing. The pressure to concentrate and perform well can cause a student to see the world around them in blinkered vision – nothing but the exam matters and the outside world mustn't intrude.

However, surely a rebellion, with shooting in the streets and looting in the shops, would penetrate the consciousness of even the most dedicated student? Well, apparently not – on Tuesday, the day after the Rising began, and by which time it was in full swing, Miss Eileen Corrigan arrived at the gate of Trinity College, ready to sit her French exam. She had somehow made her way along Harcourt Street and St Stephen's Green without noticing anything amiss, and now she waited for a porter to open the gate – which he would only do after she assured him she wasn't afraid.

In all, about 20 per cent of the candidates turned up for the exam – under twenty men and women. The test lasted from 9.30 a.m. until 5 p.m. and, she says, 'we got so much accustomed to [the firing] that we did not even lift our pens from the paper …'[1]

But if you were to explain away the students' arrival for an exam during a rebellion, by supposing that they didn't know there was a rebellion on when they left home that morning, what would you say to the idea that Miss Corrigan and others turned up again on Wednesday for another exam!

Indeed they did and this time there was no question of ignorance of events – Miss Corrigan on that day saw the body of a British soldier who had been killed by rebel snipers. Meanwhile the hall itself where the examination took place was now overlooked by houses occupied by rebels – 'so that we were really in great danger, but the sight of the hundreds of troops … gave us courage …'

Unfortunately for Miss Corrigan, the College authorities decided that so few candidates had turned up that the exam would have to be repeated when the rebellion was over. Thankfully, though, she got a good result.

34

Sackville Street or O'Connell Street?

Most published accounts of the Rising refer to Dublin's main thoroughfare as Sackville Street – some refer firstly to O'Connell Street, before adding 'or Sackville Street, as it was known in 1916'. However, the facts of the street's name aren't quite so clear-cut and while most official accounts of the time refer to events on Sackville Street, you may come across some contemporaneous reports that refer to O'Connell Street and you may naturally wonder why!

A good example of this ambiguity is found in the written submissions to the chief officer of the Dublin Corporation Fire Brigade, Thomas P. Purcell, from which he compiled the Brigade's *Annual Report* for 1916. One writer refers to Sackville Street, while another refers consistently to O'Connell Street – and at times both writers are referring not just to the same street, but to the same building on fire!

In another example an eyewitness account written soon after the rebellion refers to O'Connell Street and mentions almost in passing that: 'The official name of O'Connell

Street is Sackville Street.'[1] Rebel leader James Connolly, in several dispatches to the rebels under his command, referred to O'Connell Street.

In fact, though, changing the street's official name took some forty years!

So what was the source of this confusion? At a meeting of Dublin Corporation in December 1884, a motion to change the name of Sackville Street to O'Connell Street was carried, despite the objections of a large number of owners and occupiers of property on the street. A flurry of enraged letters were soon printed in *The Irish Times*, referring to the 'tyrannical conduct' of 'the extreme National element', and the matter went to the courts.

In July 1885, an injunction was sought and granted, 'to restrain the Lord Mayor and the Corporation of Dublin from changing the name'. Five years later the Dublin Corporation Act 1890, was enacted, with Section 42 referring to street name changes being 'at the request and subsequent to the consent of the majority in number and valuation of the ratepayers of the street'. The street's name remained unchanged as a result and so, in 1916, it was still officially called Sackville Street.

Finally in May 1924, forty years after the original motion was carried, a meeting of Dublin Corporation (successfully and without fuss) adopted the motion 'That the name of Sackville Street be, and it is hereby, changed

to O'Connell Street' in accordance with Section 42 of the
Dublin Corporation Act, 1890.

35 Lenin looks on

In July 1916, before Russia's own revolution in 1917, Vladimir Ilyich Lenin wrote approvingly of the Easter Rising in Ireland as 'a blow delivered against British imperialist bourgeois rule', and a 'heroic revolt of the most mobile and enlightened section of certain classes in an oppressed nation against its oppressors …'[1] Leon Trotsky, meanwhile, referred to '… the heroic defenders of the Dublin barricades'.[2]

Lenin continued: 'The centuries-old Irish national movement expressed itself in street fighting conducted by a section of the urban petty bourgeoisie and a section of the workers …' However, he declared that 'the misfortune of the Irish is that they have risen prematurely, when the European revolt of the proletariat has not yet matured'.

There have been many reasons put forward for the failure of the Easter Rising, but not many blame it on the immaturity of the 'European revolt of the proletariat'. At this point in history, however, we can only guess what Pearse and the other rebel leaders would have made of this particular explanation for their rebellion's unsuccessful conclusion.

36

'It wasn't Sinn Féin made the Rising – 'twas the Rising made Sinn Féin'

From the moment the firing started on Easter Monday 1916, the Easter Rising was 'blamed' on Sinn Féin, the political party founded by Arthur Griffith eleven years earlier, and the Rising became popularly known as the 'Sinn Féin Rebellion'. Indeed the 'complete and connected narrative of the Rising' as published by the *Weekly Irish Times* soon afterwards, was confidently titled the *Sinn Féin Rebellion Handbook*.

Among both civilian and military onlookers throughout the week, the labels 'rebel' and 'Sinn Féiner' were completely interchangeable – 'Stephen's Green and the Post Office are full of rebels,' one author's mother announced.

'Rebels?' he asked.

'Yes,' she replied, 'Sinn Féiners, I suppose.'[1]

Official reports also confused the two labels – in his summing-up dispatch after the rebellion, General Sir John Maxwell continually refers to 'Sinn Féiners' and the report of the Royal Commission of Inquiry into the rebellion talks at length about not just the 'Sinn Féin military movement', but even calls the Gaelic literary revival 'the Sinn Féin literary movement'. Indeed, the confusion runs even deeper, and merges the two 'movements' in a question put to Chief Secretary for Ireland Augustine Birrell: 'What turned this Sinn Féin literary movement into a military movement?'[2]

However, the fact is that the rebellion had no connection with Sinn Féin – not in its planning, nor in its execution. The Rising was planned and carried out by a group composed mainly of members of the Irish Volunteers and the Irish Citizen Army. The Irish Volunteers were founded in 1913, but following a disagreement over participation on the British side in the First World War, the organisation split into National Volunteers and Irish Volunteers, with the majority joining the National Volunteers, who favoured participation.

However, from then on, the minority Irish Volunteers began to be referred to as 'Sinn Féiners' (or 'Shinners'), although they had no links to Griffith's party, which was based 'on the principles of self-reliance, repeal of the Act of Union and the old Hungarian idea of non-recognition of the Imperial parliament'.

Of course there were probably many men who were members of both organisations, but a 'Sinn Féin' rebellion, the Easter Rising was not. The truth is that the Sinn Féin party was practically defunct by Easter 1916, yet because of the public's growing sympathy towards the rebels during and after 1916, the misnomer led to a huge change in the party's fortunes, and eventually, with a number of rebellion veterans joining its ranks (including Éamon de Valera, who replaced Griffith as president), Sinn Féin went on to win seventy-three of Ireland's 106 seats in the general election in December 1918.

37

From British gunboat to Irish patrol vessel

Pick up any book on the 1916 Easter Rising, and somewhere inside you'll read about the British gunboat *Helga*, which sailed up the mouth of the Liffey and, on Wednesday, proceeded to shell Liberty Hall, the headquarters of the Irish Transport & General Workers' Union. Considered a nest of rebel activity, it was actually empty on the day (apart from the caretaker who exited as fast as possible), but was destroyed nonetheless.

The *Helga*'s log states that she fired a total of twenty-four rounds at the Hall. Next day she fired fourteen rounds at a disused distillery tower, where Commandant Éamon de Valera had ordered a rebel flag to be placed, in a successful ruse to divert the gunship's aim away from where his men actually were – in Boland's Mills.

However, while these facts about *Helga* are fairly widely known, what may come as a surprise is to find that the *Helga* remained in Ireland after the rebellion and indeed after the First World War. Built in a Dublin dockyard, the *Helga* was launched in 1908 for use by her owners, the Department of Agriculture and Technical Instruction, as a fishery-patrol and research ship. Soon after the outbreak of the war, the *Helga* was up-gunned and taken into service as an armed patrol yacht.

After her famous role in the Rising and after the end of the First World War, the *Helga* was returned to the Department of Agriculture and Technical Instruction. Then in 1922 she came under the command of the Irish Free State, patrolling to prevent gun-running to anti-Treaty forces. In 1923 she became the property of the Department of Fisheries, reverting once again to the role of fishery-patrol and research vessel.

The *Helga* was now the *Muirchu* (Sea Hound) and sixteen years later she was once again fitted with guns and pressed into service for what became the Second World War. She saw out the Emergency and, finally, on her last voyage in 1947, her destination was the breakers' yard, but the *Helga* never arrived – a storm claimed her off the coast of Wexford.

38 Scars in stone and statue

Many decades have passed since the rebellion ended, and although not a single participant remains, there are still witnesses to the violence of that week in 1916 – witnesses that will continue to tell their tale for many decades to come.

Unfortunately these witnesses are silent ones – buildings, statues and monuments to previous wars, bearing pockmarks and holes where bullets were halted abruptly, but they can still tell a story if you look closely enough.

The best-known area for seeing this damage is along O'Connell Street, in the monument to Daniel O'Connell and in the pillars and façade of the GPO.

However, one of the most interesting places to see bullet damage from the Rising is on the façade of the College of Surgeons on St Stephen's Green, which the rebels occupied after briefly trying to defend the wide open spaces of the Green itself – a decision that had proved very costly for them. They initially tried to fortify the Green by barricading the gates and digging trenches. Author St John G. Ervine wrote: 'I heard a man say to one lad who was digging into the soft earth: "What in the name of God are you doin' there?" and the lad replied: "I don't know. I'm supposed to be diggin' a trench, but I think I'm diggin' my grave.'"

For several reasons, far fewer men than expected turned out on Easter Monday morning, and so most of the high houses and the even higher Shelbourne Hotel were left for the British to occupy – which they rapidly did, pouring rifle and machine gun fire down onto the rebels, until they quit the Green and barricaded themselves into the College of Surgeons.

Not all the rebels made it safely out of the Green though – one young rebel was shot dead just short of the railings and, as machine gun fire continued to sweep the park, his body was hit again and again, making it twitch, thereby attracting more bursts of fire.

The college itself was soon being peppered with bullets by the soldiers in the Shelbourne and the results are still visible in its façade today. Indeed, not only can the damage still be seen in the stone pillars, but the direction the bullets came from can easily be determined – the side of the pillars facing the Shelbourne is pockmarked, while the other side isn't.

More damage can be seen nearby on Fusiliers' Arch, the memorial arch which forms the Grafton Street entrance to St Stephen's Green, and this damage also obviously came from the direction of the Shelbourne Hotel.

However, although Ervine saw that many of the Shelbourne's windows were 'full of bullet-holes', you'll have a hard time finding damage in the hotel's brickwork today – it would seem that granite has a better 'memory' for bullets than brick.

Another location which bears the scars and memories of back-and-forth gunfire is near Mount Street Bridge. Here also, the rebels were at a height disadvantage after soldiers occupied the bell tower of St Mary's church on Haddington Road, from where they were able to fire down at the rebels occupying Clanwilliam House and 25 Northumberland Road. Clanwilliam House burned down, but No. 25 still stands and on its granite corner blocks bullet marks can still be seen, while high up on the church tower, more bullet damage is visible – mainly on the side facing Mount Street Bridge.

39

Scars in wood

Stone, brick and metal can all present solid, unmoving, reminders of the bullets that went back and forth during the rebellion – bullets aimed at people, but which found inanimate targets instead. But scars can still be seen elsewhere, as well as on buildings and statues, and sometimes in the most unexpected places.

The area in and around Mount Street Bridge in south Dublin was the site of the bloodiest battle of the entire Easter Rising. Its tale has been told in many books, but there are sides to it that are little known or have never been told.

Ms Dorothy May Kerr Johnston was cycling with her father (the 'Johnston' of Johnston, Mooney & O'Brien bakery fame and one of the defenders of Trinity College – *see Fact 47*) on Dublin's northside on Easter Monday 1916, and she had some interesting experiences while trying to get back to her southside home after the rebellion had broken out. As it happened, home for the Johnstons was Percy Place, a road which fronts onto the Grand Canal and at one end of which is Mount Street Bridge.

Compared to her experiences getting across the city, by going home, Ms Johnston was jumping from the frying pan into the fire: her family spent most of the Battle of Mount Street Bridge in an outbuilding at the end of the garden. And just as well – windows that hadn't been smashed by bullet before Thursday were soon shattered by the blast of artillery, as a naval gun, now mounted on a lorry and positioned in Percy Place, opened fire on rebels lodged in Boland's Mills (*see Fact 28*).

On the same day, twenty-nine-year-old Charles Hachette Hyland of No. 3 Percy Place, who had risked his life several times the day before by helping carry wounded under fire, was simply looking out his garden gate when he was shot dead.

And while Ms Johnston was sheltering, bullets were flying into her house – including one which entered a writing desk and is still there to this day.

Also still to be seen today are the remnants of bullet damage caused inside the schoolhouse on the south side of Mount Street Bridge, which, when attacked by the soldiers, didn't contain a single rebel – the Volunteers had occupied it earlier, but vacated the position very shortly after. Today the building is a bar/restaurant/hotel, and the rebellion damage can still be clearly seen in part of the wooden ceiling of the bar.

40 Scars in paper

During the Battle of Mount Street Bridge, Captain Arthur Annan Dickson of the Sherwood Foresters Regiment was out on the street with his men, in the thick of the fighting – and his memoirs tell a grim story of a bloody battle indeed:

> … shots came from a house in the road-fork just ahead … I broke in with a few bayonet-men but the rebels left by the back way … I heard that my friend Hawken had been killed in attacking a house at a cross-roads farther on. That house was blown in with bombs and the rebels gradually gave back from house to house as we advanced by rushes with some cover from trees along the kerbs, with bullets of all sorts chipping pavements and gate-posts; one chipped the bark one side of a tree as I left it. Another must have ricocheted off the pavement and struck end-on into my Field Service Pocket Book in a side pocket, but I never noticed it till afterwards … We had to bomb a school building that the rebels were holding, and one of my men, Irvine, did some good throwing, right through the windows …

Captain Dickson's pocketbook survives to this day, preserved in London's Imperial War Museum and bearing what must be one of the most remarkable scars of the rebellion.

Meanwhile, across town in Marsh's Library, beside St Patrick's cathedral, books belonging to the collection of Marsh's first librarian, Dr Elias Bouhéreau, sat quietly on shelves as they had done for hundreds of years. Dr Bouhéreau was a Huguenot refugee who, having fled persecution in France in 1695, settled in Ireland, bringing his books with him.

Unfortunately, with rebels in Jacob's factory, and British troops camped in the park beside St Patrick's cathedral, Marsh's Library found itself in the firing line during the Easter Rising. On Sunday morning the peace of the Library was shattered when a British machine gunner peppered the building – glass was shattered, wood was splintered and several of Dr Bouhéreau's ancient books, which had survived the flight from France, were pierced, including *La Discipline des Eglises Réformées de France* by Isaac d'Huisseau, printed exactly 250 years previously in 1666. The books are still in Marsh's Library today, having returned to their former quiet existence, although now bearing permanent reminders of the Easter Rising.

41 Executing his orders

If the bullet that lodged in Captain Arthur Dickson's pocket-book had gone a bit further, then that would have been the end of his part in the 1916 rebellion.

In fact Captain Dickson went on to perform a role that was traditionally kept secret – however, thanks to his memoirs, we know the procedure that was followed in the execution of the rebel leaders and we know the identity of the officer who commanded one of the fourteen firing squads that carried out the death sentences in Kilmainham Gaol – Captain Dickson himself.

His recollections were written in the early 1920s, not long after the events in Dublin in 1916, and are worth repeating in full:

> A kindly but strict old Major … gave detailed instructions:
> I was to march my firing-squad of a Sergeant and twelve men to a space cut off from the execution-point by a projecting wall; halt them to ground arms there; march them forward twelve paces to halt with their backs to their rifles, each of which I was then to load and replace on the ground. Thus no man knew whether his rifle had

been loaded with blank or with ball; each was therefore left not knowing whether he personally had shot the man or not. The men were then [to be] marched back to pick up their rifles and hold them, at attention under my eye, until word came that the prisoner was to be led out; they must then be marched round and halted facing the execution wall.

'A priest will accompany the prisoner,' the Major told me, 'and as the priest leaves him, you give the orders – Ready; Present; Fire.' Then, he emphasised, 'the men must not remain in sight of the prisoner: immediately you turn them about and march them back around the baffle wall. There they ground arms, you march them forward to halt facing away, while you empty the breech of each rifle and collect the cartridge cases, all to be handed in after. Then march them back to pick up their rifles, clean them on the spot and the job is done.'

We marched our squads to [Kilmainham Gaol] long before dawn in a dismal drizzle, but the men with memories of our losses seemed to have no qualms as to doing the job. 'Pity to dirty all these rifles; why can't we do him in with a bit of bayonet practice?' We had to wait while it grew faintly light and I took the chance to instruct the squad exactly what orders they would get; I didn't want any muddle about getting them back around that wall.

After 'Ready!' I told them, 'on the word "Present", you bring your rifles smartly up to the standing-aim position, aiming at a piece of white paper pinned on his chest and on the word "Fire" – steady pressure on the trigger, just like on the range. Then, at once, I shall give you "Slope arms" – "About turn"; then as we clear this wall – "Right incline" – "Halt" – "Ground arms".'

Thanks to that preparation, it was carried out smoothly. The thirteen rifles went off in a single volley. The rebel dropped to the ground like an empty sack; I barked out 'Slope ARMS: About TURN; Quick MARCH!' They marched in perfect order round that wall, grounded arms, and I told them 'Right: you made a good job of that, gentlemen'; remember, we had all lost some good pals in our first days' active service. I can't say I felt much else except that it was just another job that had to be done …'[1]

Dickson's firing party carried out their duty on 8 May, so the executed rebel was either Éamonn Ceannt, Michael Mallin, Seán Heuston or Con Colbert.

Like much of Dickson's memoirs, the description of the execution by firing squad is written quite matter-of-factly, except when it comes to the final paragraph, when he writes: '… I was glad there was no doubt the rifles had done their work and there was no need for me to do what that old Major had told me, about the officer going back and finishing the job off with his revolver.'

42 Lucky escapes

With bullets flying and fires raging, and a high proportion of the young combatants seeing action for the first time, it is no surprise that some of them did whatever it took to avoid joining the lengthening list of casualties. There are many examples of soldiers and rebels breaking down under the pressure of combat (and in some cases killing their own comrades), but two tales of British soldiers taking desperate measures to avoid becoming casualties are worth mentioning in particular.

At the South Dublin Union (now St James's Hospital) fierce fighting took place during the week of the rebellion, some of it hand-to-hand. The Union was a large sprawling complex of buildings, with some occupied by rebels and others by soldiers. One of these was the bakehouse, occupied by the British until Thursday when, fearing that they were in a death trap, they waited until nightfall and, having removed their boots to prevent noise, rushed across a courtyard to a more secure position.

For some unknown reason, however, one soldier was left behind, along with the dead body of a comrade. Next morning, when a hearse belonging to the South Dublin Union arrived to remove the body, it contained two coffins. The stranded soldier, seeing an opportunity, promptly got in and the lid was put over him.

Safely inside, the erstwhile target was carried through the Union grounds out of the danger zone to the Rialto end of the complex, where 'he rose from his temporary resting place, to the consternation of the spectators'.[1] Later on, the soldier literally had a captive audience, when he told the story of his escape to Volunteers detained in Richmond Barracks.

Meanwhile two other soldiers who had been held captive in the GPO by the rebels during the week of the rebellion, had an escape of a different sort – an unnecessary escape, as it turned out. The two, Sergeant Henry and Private Doyle, had been released by the rebels during the general evacuation of the GPO when the fires in the building got out of control on Friday.

The post office evacuation was conducted through the Henry Street exit and, with the street under heavy gunfire, it would seem that the pair ducked into the Coliseum Theatre, which was a mere 25 metres or so down the road. And having made it safely inside, there they stayed. Outside, meanwhile, the rebellion came to an end two days later, on Sunday.

Three more days passed before, eventually, on the following

Wednesday, the hungry and dishevelled Sergeant Henry and Private Doyle were discovered still hiding in the burned ruins of the theatre, utterly unaware that the fighting had ended and the danger had passed.

43

From broadcasting rebel to Quiet Man

In 1916, twenty-year-old Arthur Shields was a Volunteer with the GPO garrison and during the rebellion he played a part in the occupation of the Dublin Wireless School of Telegraphy on O'Connell Street (*see Fact 16*). However, it could be said that 'Volunteer' in the Easter Rising wasn't the first role Shields had played – tellingly, his entry in the list of prisoners 'removed from Richmond Barracks, Dublin, on April 30th, and lodged in Knutsford Detention Barracks, England, on May 1st' gives his profession as 'actor'.

Already an experienced actor with the Abbey Theatre, Shields went on to become a well-known character player on Broadway and in Hollywood, with perhaps his best-known role being that of Rev. Dr Cyril Playfair in *The Quiet Man*, in the company of his famous brother Barry Fitzgerald, along with John Wayne and Maureen O'Hara.

Interestingly, another famous movie that Arthur Shields starred in was *How Green Was My Valley* (1941), in which he played alongside John Loder, another Easter Rising veteran, but from the British side (*see Fact 44*). The pair also appeared on the cast list of two other movies, and it is tempting to think that at some stage they may have swapped reminiscences of the real-life drama they played their parts in, in Dublin 1916.

44 From Dublin to Hollywood

One of the most famous and commonly reproduced photographs taken during the Rising is of the moment of Pearse's surrender on Saturday, 29 April. In fact, it is such a familiar image that in some respects it has lost its impact, yet there probably aren't many rebellions whose moment of collapse is photographically recorded for posterity.

The picture shows the Commander of Dublin Forces in Ireland, Brigadier General W.H.M. Lowe, facing a clearly un-humbled P.H. Pearse, who is offering his surrender. On Pearse's right, but almost entirely obscured, is Elizabeth O'Farrell (a nurse with Cumann na mBan), who carried the subsequent surrender dispatches to rebel commandants.

Meanwhile, on the left of the photo, to Brigadier Lowe's right, is his aide-de-camp and son, Major John Lowe. It was to him that Brigadier Lowe dictated his negative response to Pearse's initial message wishing to negotiate a ceasefire (and in which, by his own admission, John Lowe spelled Pearse's name incorrectly).

Pearse subsequently surrendered unconditionally and Major Lowe was ordered by his father to take Pearse to

Kilmainham Gaol, accompanied by another officer and an armed guard.

However, John Lowe's army service didn't end in Ireland; apart from Dublin in 1916, he saw service in Gallipoli, Egypt and the Somme, before being taken prisoner by the Germans in 1918. When the First World War ended, Lowe then used his new knowledge of German to start a pickle business, but it quickly folded. Then, on the suggestion of a friend, he tried his hand, with some minor success, at being a movie actor in the German film industry – a path which eventually led Lowe to change his name to keep his acting career quiet from his disapproving father.

So John Lowe became John Loder, eventually moving to Hollywood, California, where he gained some fame in movies and on stage and TV (even at times acting alongside a rebel veteran of the Easter Rising – *see Fact 43*). In 1929, he appeared in Paramount Studios' first 'talking' picture and in subsequent years married five times – one of his wives being the famous beauty Hedy Lamarr.

45 Dublin Mean Time vs Greenwich Mean Time

From 1880 until 1916, Ireland and Great Britain maintained different time zones – Great Britain of course followed Greenwich Mean Time (GMT), but Ireland followed Dublin Mean Time (DMT), which was a precise 25 minutes behind GMT.

The 'Statutes (Definition of Time) Act, 1880', which legally defined the difference between GMT and DMT, was superseded by the 'Time (Ireland) Act, 1916', which was: 'An Act to assimilate the Time adopted for use in Ireland to that adopted for use in Great Britain'. In other words, DMT was abolished.

This change came into effect on 1 October 1916 (some sources say the change happened on 23 August 1916, but that was the date of Royal Assent for the Act, not the date on which the change came into effect).

However, the Rising began months earlier on 24 April 1916, at approximately 12 o'clock – Dublin Mean Time. Therefore, when modern commemorations of 1916 begin at midday outside the GPO, they are actually 25 minutes early!

46 Who's going to pay for all this?

There can often be a tendency, when looking back at historic events, to consider just the event itself, without looking in too much detail at its consequences, other than in broad generalisations. However, looking at the after-effects of an event can often shed new light on the event itself – an interesting example is the 'Defence of the Realm Losses Royal Commission'.

This was a body set up by Royal commission in 1916 (while the First World War was still raging) 'to consider and report what compensation should be paid in respect of losses incurred through the exercise by the Crown of its rights and duties in the Defence of the Realm'. As applied to the rebellion in Ireland, this referred to losses and damages caused to civilian property by the army while suppressing the revolt.

Many claims were considered by the commissioners, right up until 1920, and a proportion of those claims were indeed for damages caused by the suppression of the Easter Rising.

One example was case number 4529, that of P. Donnelly

and Sons, coal merchants, whose offices in 29 Lower Sackville Street were destroyed by fire. Their claim, made in 1918, was based on the fire being caused 'by the explosion of shells fired by the military into the Post Office held by the rebels ... exactly opposite' their offices.

They claimed that among the items destroyed were their account books, containing about 2,000 debtors' names and details, and that, at the date of the fire, they were owed £12,382 by these debtors. Having 'applied to every debtor whose name was within their recollection', they had recovered £3,877, leaving them short the balance of £8,505, which they now claimed from the commissioners.

In the legalistic language of the commission's reported judgement, things start out well for P. Donnelly and Sons. Despite being disputed by the military, the commission decided to 'assume that the act of interference has been established' – in other words, that the fire was a result of military action.

Unfortunately it's all downhill from there. The commission found that the debts owed were still owing – 'What the fire destroyed was not the debts, but the written record ... of the debts.' For that, and other reasons, the claim was rejected, although the coal merchants were awarded £21 towards the expenses of preparing the application.

Interestingly, by way of a possible explanation for the late date of the coal merchants' application, it is worth noting that another body which considered compensation claims arising from the rebellion was the 'Property Losses (Ireland) Committee', set up in June 1916 – it seems that P. Donnelly and Sons had already submitted their claim to this committee, but it was also rejected there.

47 Rebellion's silver lining

The complex of buildings, gardens and open spaces that comprise Trinity College Dublin today is not only fairly large, but also situated right in the heart of Dublin city and although the college has expanded since 1916, even back then it made up a significant part of the city centre. As such, it was inevitable that it would play a major role in the rebellion and whichever side controlled its acres would simultaneously exert control over a swathe of the surrounding buildings and streets.

At the same time as the GPO was being occupied by the rebels at the start of the rebellion, the entire TCD campus contained only eight armed men (members of its Officers Training Corps or OTC) and could easily have been over-run. However, the rebels made no move on the college – it may or may not have featured in their plans, but regardless, because of the confusion surrounding the call to rebellion, the number of men that would have been needed to occupy it simply was not available.

Whatever the rebels' plans, the college staff lost no time in rounding up absent members of the OTC and 'stray' soldiers (mostly colonials on leave from France) were pressed into service, with the result that by 7 p.m. on the first day of the Rising, the number of defenders had risen to about 150. From then on, the rebel strongholds in the GPO and St Stephen's Green areas were virtually cut off from each other, with messengers coming under fire from the college rooftops (*see Fact 14*).

By Tuesday evening, regular troops had begun to arrive and over the coming days the college played host to 4,000 soldiers and a large number of horses, as well as numerous artillery pieces.

However, the quick action of the OTC and the contribution of its members, along with college staff and colonial soldiers, wasn't overlooked when the fighting was over. Their actions were seen to have prevented the rebel takeover of the college, thereby saving the surrounding houses and businesses from looting and destruction.

The loyal citizens' appreciation 'materialised by subscription into a fund, exceeding £700',[1] and a number of items of silver were purchased and presented to the College and its defenders on 5 August 1916. Two large cups were presented to the provost and miniature replicas were awarded to about 170 OTC members, staff and colonials.

Not every recipient was present, however – for example Private Garnet D. King of the 4th Regiment South African (Scottish) Infantry was in hospital in England, having been wounded in the abdomen on Wednesday, 26 April. Indeed, Private King never did see his reward – he was later wounded in the shoulder and again in the abdomen while in France. He died and was buried in France almost exactly a year after the rebellion began in Dublin.

Meanwhile, among the OTC cadets who did receive their cups was J.K. Johnston, of 'Johnston, Mooney & O'Brien' bakery fame and father of Ms Dorothy May Kerr Johnston (*see Fact 39*).

48 Final shots ...

As explained in Fact 3, the Volunteers in Laois have a good claim to the first shot of the Rising – but the last shot is, unsurprisingly, a bit more difficult to attribute.

Probably the last offensive action by the rebels took place at Sybil Head in County Kerry on the evening of Monday, 1 May. A signal station on the outer edge of the Dingle Peninsula, Sybil Head had been hurriedly garrisoned by a platoon of Royal Marines with a machine gun, and although the attack was 'met with heavy fire', the rebels escaped.

However, the last unofficial (i.e. rebel) shot was probably fired in the streets of Dublin by a sniper acting alone, either unwittingly or deliberately in ignorance of the ceasefire (*see Fact 31*).

On the other side, if we don't include the executions of the rebel leaders, then the last official action by the British which resulted in casualties was probably the attempted arrest on 2 May of the Kent brothers near Fermoy in County Cork – an operation which went horribly wrong and led to the death of a policeman and the fatal shooting of one of the Kents.

As part of the 'tidying-up' operations around the country-side following the rebel surrender, a party of constables from the Royal Irish Constabulary arrived at the Kent home at 3.45 a.m. Head Constable Rowe kicked at the door and demanded that it be opened so they could arrest Thomas and David Kent, two prominent local dissidents. Shots were fired from the house and Rowe was killed – a gun battle then ensued, lasting for an hour until the family offered to surrender. When they came out of the house, another Kent brother, Richard, made a run for it, but was fatally wounded.

Thomas, David and William Kent were court-martialled, and although the raid on their house was related, but separate, to the actual rebellion, they were charged with having taken part in 'armed rebellion'. William was acquitted and David was given a five-year prison sentence. However, Thomas was executed in Cork Detention Barracks on 9 May. Years later, Cork's railway station was renamed the Thomas Kent station.

49 How hot off the presses?

These days, with the Internet, digital imaging, and so on, we're pretty fast when it comes to delivering the news 'as it happens'. Obviously in 1916, the media weren't quite as quick, but, as ever, where there is a demand, there will soon be a supply – and the demand for information and pictures about the Easter Rising was enormous.

Indeed, many people were so eager to find out what was going on, that they put themselves in harm's way, sometimes with fatal results (*see Fact 10*). But the majority of people were happy to wait for newspapers, books and souvenir booklets to tell and to show them what had happened that Easter Week, and they didn't have to wait long.

Of course, newspapers were back on the streets of Dublin as soon as the rebellion was suppressed (some early copies being rented instead of sold!), but it may be surprising to learn how quickly books and souvenir albums were produced.

Within two months, there were 'complete' accounts available, at very varied prices:

- *The Irish Rebellion of 1916: A brief history of the revolt and its suppression*, by John F. Boyle – 4 shillings and 6 pence
- *The Irish Rebellion: What Happened and Why*, by F.A. McKenzie – 1 shilling

And if pictures were what you wanted instead of words, then within two months you could choose from:

- *The Record of the Irish Rebellion of 1916*, from the publishers of *Irish Life* – 1 shilling
- *Dublin and the 'Sinn Féin Rising'* from Wilson Hartnell & Co. – 9 pence
- *The Sinn Féin Revolt Illustrated*, by Hely's – 1 shilling
- *Dublin After the Six Days' Insurrection – thirty-one pictures from the camera of Mr T.W. Murphy* – 7 pence

By year's end then, a mere eight months after the Rising had ended, there were at least nine additions to the list, not to mention numerous in-depth articles and analyses in various periodicals, magazines and newspapers on both sides of the Atlantic and as far away as Australia. From *Popular Mechanics* published in Chicago, to *Le Panorama de la Guerre*, in Paris, media around the world took time out from covering the First World War to bring their readers news of a small rebellion against an enormous Empire.

50 And finally ...

There are many, many more facts and stories out there than could possibly appear in this or in any (indeed *all*) books on the Easter Rising, but I've tried to include as many as possible. Here though, are some very short facts that didn't fit anywhere else, but that are worth mentioning!

- During Easter Week, in Dublin at least, the weather was so consistently good that 'Rebellion weather' was a phrase in use for years afterwards. (Of course, the 'extraordinarily fine' weather had its drawbacks, as 'it made it imperative to allow as little time as possible to elapse between death and burial' – *see Fact 32*).

- Throughout the Easter Rising, the rebels sang many songs, whether to keep their morale up, to send a signal to their enemies, or just for the enjoyment of it. However, one song in particular became associated with the rebellion and the defiance of the rebels – it was to become Ireland's national anthem, *The Soldier's Song*. In just one example, as the remaining garrison left the blazing inferno that the GPO had become, 'The amazing thing was that, as they marched towards the exit, they sang. As the flames ... were threatening to bring in the roof on their heads ... they roared out *The Soldier's Song* as one man.'[1] Today the anthem is known by its Irish title, *Amhrán na bhFiann*, but what most people don't realise is that when Peadar Kearney wrote the song in 1907, he wrote it in English. It was many years before it was translated into Irish and until then it was sung in English – even in the GPO in Easter 1916.

- At a meeting of the Bank of Ireland's Court of Directors on 18 May 1916, several Rising-related claims for payment were noted, including one for 'Four Charred £1 Notes' by a Mr R. Matheson, solicitor, as well as another for 'Twelve £1 Notes forwarded by English Banks in letters ... believed to have been destroyed in the Post Office, Dublin.'

- A few days earlier, in the same bank's notes for a general board meeting of 12 May 1916, it is recorded that one Isaac J. Kelly of the College Green office 'has not resumed duty since the Easter holidays'. This is marked as 'Noted'. Meanwhile, in the prisoner lists in the *Sinn Féin Rebellion Handbook*, we can find one Isaac Kelly transported to Knutsford Detention Barracks on 3 May – his occupation is given as 'bank clerk'. Isaac doesn't seem to feature in the rebellion's Roll of Honour, though, but there is a 'Kelly' noted as having fought in the St Stephen's Green area, with no first name given, so perhaps that is our missing bank clerk!

- A writer with the *Ballymena Observer*, Bab M'Keen (the pen name of John Weir), was a reluctant witness to events in O'Connell Street during the rebellion, being stranded in the Granville Hotel, and he later told his readers about his experiences. Writing, as he did, in Ulster Scots, he describes one incident involving a hotel employee called Daisy. 'She was yin o' the waitresses, a very nice wee lass ' at ivery body liked, an' yin evenin' juist efther tay yin o' the big guns at the heid o' the street was let aff at the Post Office wi' a soun' like the brustin' o' a plenet 'at frichtened the hale o' us an' afore you cud wink, doon draps Daisy in a deid faint, onther the table.'

- In the Battle of Mount Street Bridge, after the shooting from No.1 Clanwilliam Place had stopped, the fires took over and, having suffered the weight of many hours' gunfire and bombing, the house was ablaze, burning so brightly that it could be seen for miles. In his report for 1916, the chief of the Dublin Fire Brigade notes: 'Wednesday ... 1 and 2 Clanwilliam Place – Did not attend as the houses were being shelled by the military.' Unsurprisingly, therefore, when No. 2 caught fire and the residents, Mr and Mrs Mathis, emerged from their basement hiding place, they had no choice but to sit in their back garden on deck chairs and watch their home burn.

Endnotes

Fact 1

1. Chatterton, *Danger Zone: The Story of the Queenstown Command*.

Fact 3

1. The names recorded on the memorial are:
Eamon Fleming, O/C; Patrick J. Ramsbottom, Vice O/C;
Lorcan O'Brádaig, QM; Thomas F. Brady; Michael Gray;
Patrick Muldowney; John Frawley; John Muldowney; Colum
Holohan; Michael Walsh; Terence Byrne; James Ramsbottom;
Patrick J. Fleming; Noreen Brady; Michael J. Sheridan;
Kathleen Brady; Seán Maguire; May Conroy; Breda Conroy

Fact 4

1. *Capuchin Annual, The*, Dublin, 1966.

Fact 5

1. *An t-Óglách: The Army Journal*, 10 April, 1926.

Fact 6

1. *An t-Óglách*, 16 January, 1926.

2. Caulfield, *The Easter Rebellion*.

3. McHugh, *Dublin 1916*.

4. Fitzpatrick, *Trinity College and Irish Society 1914–1922*.

Fact 7

1. Good, *Enchanted by Dreams: The journal of a revolutionary*.

2. Caulfield, *The Easter Rebellion*.
3. Good, *Enchanted by Dreams*.

Fact 8

1. Ervine, *The story of the Irish rebellion*.
2. O'Higgins, *The Soldier's Story of Easter Week*.
3. *Sinn Féin Rebellion Handbook*.

Fact 9

1. McHugh, *Dublin 1916*.

Fact 10

1. McHugh, *Dublin 1916*.
2. Brennan-Whitmore, *Dublin Burning: The Easter Rising from behind the barricades*.
3. Good, *Enchanted by Dreams*.
4. Redmond-Howard, *Six Days of the Irish Republic*.
5. *Ibid*.
6. Foy and Barton, *The Easter Rising*.
7. Lyntton, *An Innocent Bysinger*.
8. Caulfield, *The Easter Rebellion*.

Fact 11

1. Good, *Enchanted by Dreams*.
2. O'Rahilly, *Winding the Clock – O'Rahilly and the 1916 Rising*.

Fact 13

1. Greaves, *Liam Mellows and the Irish Revolution*.

Fact 14

1. Joly, *Reminiscences & Anticipations*.

Fact 16

1.   Fisher, *Broadcasting in Ireland*.

Fact 17

1.   Redmond-Howard, *Six Days of the Irish Republic*.

Fact 18

1.   Brennan-Whitmore, *Dublin Burning: The Easter Rising from behind the barricades*.

Fact 22

1.   Redmond-Howard, *Six Days of the Irish Republic*.
2.   Foy and Barton, *The Easter Rising*.

Fact 23

1.   Chatterton, *Danger Zone*.

Fact 24

1.   Stephens, *The Insurrection in Dublin*.
2.   The story behind J.F. Foster's death is unknown, he is just another name in the list of 250 victims buried in Glasnevin. However, the *Sinn Féin Rebellion Handbook* does say that the 250 deaths 'were directly attributable to the Rising' and that they 'occurred as a result of bullet or gunshot wounds arising out of the rebellion'. It also adds that the list includes 'several persons who were trampled to death by crowds in the street'.

Fact 27

1.   Hamilton Norway, *The Sinn Féin Rebellion as They Saw It*.
2.   Gibbon, *Inglorious Soldier*.
3.   *AFV News*, Jan-Apr 2000, Vol. 35, No. 1 (Ontario, 2000).
4.   *Ibid*.

5.   Hamilton Norway, *The Sinn Féin Rebellion as They Saw It*.

Fact 28

1.   Brunicardi, Daire, *The Sea Hound – the story of an Irish ship*.

Fact 29

1.   Caulfield, *The Easter Rebellion*.
2.   Griffith and O'Grady, *Curious Journey: An oral history of Ireland's unfinished revolution*.

Fact 30

1.   Royal Commission on the Arrest and Subsequent Treatment of Mr Francis Sheehy-Skeffington, Mr Thomas Dickson, and Mr Patrick James McIntyre.
2.   Caulfield, *The Easter Rebellion*.
3.   Kildea, *Called to arms: Australian soldiers in the Easter Rising 1916*.
4.   Gibbon, *Inglorious Soldier*.

Fact 31

1.   Hamilton Norway, *The Sinn Féin Rebellion as They Saw It*.
2.   Joy, *The Irish Rebellion of 1916 and its Martyrs: Erin's tragic Easter*.

Fact 32

1.   Kildea, *Called to arms: Australian soldiers in the Easter Rising 1916*.
2.   'Experiences of a VAD at Dublin Castle during the Rebellion', *Blackwood's Magazine*, December 1916.
3.   *Capuchin Annual, The*, 1966.
4.   Redmond-Howard, *Six Days of the Irish Republic*.

Fact 33

1.   Fitzpatrick, *Trinity College and Irish Society 1914-1922.*

Fact 34

1.   Ervine, *The story of the Irish rebellion.*

Fact 35

1.   Lenin, *On Britain.*
2.   Trotsky, *Trotsky's Writings on Britain.*

Fact 36

1.   Taaffe, *Those Days are Gone Away.*
2.   Royal Commission on the Rebellion in Ireland – Report of Commission.

Fact 41

1.   Taken from www.derbyshirelads.uwclub.nct/Men/
     aa dickson–memoirs.htm

Fact 42

1.   *Capuchin Annual, The,* 1966.

Fact 47

1.   *Sinn Féin Rebellion Handbook.*

Fact 50

1.   *An t-Óglách,* 20 March 1926.

Bibliography

This bibliography is not a comprehensive list of publications concerning the Easter Rising 1916, but comprises those works referred to in the text, along with some publications recommended by the author for readers interested in further study of the period.

Primary sources:

Diary of Seosamh de Brún
Diary of Bella Glockler

Printed sources

1916 Rebellion Handbook (Mourne River Press, 1998)

Barton, Brian, *From Behind a Closed Door: Secret court martial records of the 1916 Easter Rising* (Belfast, 2002)

Beesly, Patrick, *Room 40: British Naval Intelligence 1914–1918* (Oxford, 1984)

Brennan-Whitmore, W.J., *Dublin Burning: The Easter Rising from behind the barricades* (Dublin, 1996)

Brunicardi, Daire, *The Sea Hound – the story of an Irish ship* (Cork, 2001)

Carrothers, John Samuel, *Memoirs of A Young Lieutenant, 1898–1917* (Enniskillen, n.d.)

Carty, James, *Bibliography of Irish History 1912–1921* (Dublin, 1936)

Caulfield, Max, *The Easter Rebellion* (Dublin, 1995)

Chatterton, E. Keble, *Danger Zone: The Story of the Queenstown Command* (London, 1934)

Coates, Tim (series ed.), *The Irish Uprising 1914–1921: papers from the British parliamentary archive* (London, 2000)

Coffey, Thomas M., *Agony at Easter: The 1916 Irish uprising* (London, 1969)

Connell, Joseph E.A., Jnr, *Where's Where in Dublin: A Directory of Historic Locations 1913–1923* (Dublin 2006)

Connolly, Nora, *The Irish Rebellion of 1916 or the Unbroken Tradition* (New York, 1919)

Coogan, Tim Pat, *1916: The Easter Rising* (London, 2001)

Cosgrave, Maurice, *A Brief History of the General Post Office Dublin* (Dublin, 1991)

de Búrca, Séamus, *The Soldier's Song: The Story of Peadar Ó Cearnaigh* (Dublin, 1957)

de Courcy Ireland, John, *The Sea and the Easter Rising* (Dublin, 1996)

Defence of the Realm Losses Royal Commission, First-Fifth Reports of the Commissioners (HM Stationery Office, 1916-1920)

Doherty, Gabriel and Keogh, Dermot (eds), *1916 - The Long Revolution* (Cork, 2007)

Dublin's Fighting Story 1916-1921: Told by the men who made it (Tralee, n.d.)

Duff, Charles, *Six Days to Shake an Empire* (London, 1966)

Ebenezer, Lyn, *Fron-goch and the birth of the IRA* (Llanrwst, 2006)

Ervine, St John G., "The story of the Irish rebellion', in *Century Magazine*, 1917

Ferguson, Stephen, *Self Respect and a Little Extra Leave: GPO Staff in 1916* (Dublin, 2005)

Fisher, Desmond, *Broadcasting in Ireland* (Routledge, 1978)

FitzGerald, Desmond, *Desmond's Rising: Memoirs 1913 to Easter 1916* (Dublin, 2006)

Fitzpatrick, Georgina, *Trinity College and Irish Society 1914-1922* (Dublin, 1992)

Foy, Michael and Barton, Brian, *The Easter Rising* (Stroud, 1999)

Gibbon, Monk, *Inglorious Soldier* (London, 1968)

Githens-Mazer, Jonathan, *Myths and Memories of the Easter Rising: Cultural and Political Nationalism in Ireland* (Dublin, 2006)

Good, Joe, *Enchanted by Dreams: The journal of a revolutionary* (Dingle, 1996)

Greaves, C. Desmond, *Liam Mellows and the Irish Revolution* (London, 1971)

Griffith, Kenneth and O'Grady, Timothy, *Curious Journey: An oral history of Ireland's unfinished revolution* (Cork, 1998)

Hamilton Norway, Mary Louisa and Arthur, *The Sinn Féin Rebellion as They Saw It* (Dublin, 1999)

Hegarty, Shane and O'Toole, Fintan, *The Irish Times book of the 1916 Rising* (Dublin, 2006)

Heuston, John M., OP, *Headquarters Battalion Easter Week 1916* (Dublin, 1966)

Hogan, Robert and O'Neill, Michael J. (eds), *Joseph Holloway's Abbey Theatre: A selection from his unpublished journal Impressions of a Dublin Playgoer* (London and Amsterdam, 1967)

Holt, Edgar, *Protest in Arms: The Irish troubles 1916-1923* (York, 1961)

Hopkinson, Michael (ed.), *Frank Henderson's Easter Rising: Recollections of a Dublin Volunteer* (Cork, 1998)

Hutton, Louise, *Every Little Breeze* (Dublin, 2001)

Introduction to The Bureau of Military History 1913-1921, An (Military Archives, 2002)

Irwin, Wilmot, *Betrayal in Ireland: An eye-witness record of the tragic and terrible years of Revolution and Civil War in Ireland 1916-24* (Belfast, n.d.)

Jackdaw No. 61, *The Easter Rising: Dublin 1916*, Jackdaw Publications Document Pack (London, 1969)

Jeffery, Keith, *The GPO and the Easter Rising* (Dublin, 2006)

Joly, J., *Reminiscences & Anticipations* (London, 1920)

Joy, Maurice (ed.), *The Irish Rebellion of 1916 and its Martyrs: Erin's tragic Easter* (New York, 1916)

Kerry's Fighting Story 1916-1921: Told by the men who made it (Tralee, n.d.)

Kildea, Jeff, 'Called to arms: Australian soldiers in the Easter Rising 1916', in *Journal of the Australian War Memorial* 39 (Australian War Memorial & Australian National University, 2003)

Lenin, V.I., *On Britain* (Moscow, n.d.)

Limerick's Fighting Story From 1916 to the Truce with Britain (Tralee, n.d.)

Loder, John, *Hollywood Hussar, the life and times of John Loder* (London, 1977)

London Gazette, *Report from Gen. Maxwell on Dublin Rebellion*, 21 July 1916

Lynch, Diarmuid, *The IRB and the 1916 Insurrection* (Cork, 1957)

Lytton, Sir Henry, *A Wandering Minstrel* (London, 1933)

MacEntee, Seán, *Episode at Easter* (Dublin, 1966)

McHugh, Roger (ed.), *Dublin 1916* (London, 1976)

M'Keen, Bab, *Wi' The Sinn Féiners in Dublin – Bab M'Keen's experience,* reprinted from *Ballymena Observer,* 5 and 12 May, 1916, revised second edition, NP (1916)

Nevinson, H.W., *Last Changes, Last Chances* (London, 1928)

O'Brien, Paul, *Blood on the Streets* (Cork, 2008)

Ó Broin, Leon, *Dublin Castle and the 1916 Rising: The story of Sir Matthew Nathan* (Dublin, 1967)

Ó Dubhghaill, M., *Insurrection Fires at Eastertide: A Golden Jubilee anthology of the Easter Rising* (Cork, 1966)

O'Farrell, Mick, *A Walk Through Rebel Dublin 1916* (Dublin, 1999)

O'Higgins, Brian, *The Soldier's Story of Easter Week* (Dublin, 1966)

Ó Maitiú, Séamas, *W&R Jacob – Celebrating 150 years of Irish biscuit making* (Dublin, 2001)

O'Mahony, Seán, *Frongoch: University of Revolution* (Killiney, 1987)

O'Rahilly, Aodogán, *Winding the Clock – O'Rahilly and the 1916 Rising* (Dublin, 1991)

Oates, Lieut Colonel W.C., *The Sherwood Foresters in the Great War 1914–1918 – the 2/8th* (Nottingham, 1920)

Rebel Cork's Fighting Story From 1916 to the Truce with Britain (Tralee, n.d.)

Redmond-Howard, L.G., *Six Days of the Irish Republic* (Boston, 1916)

Reilly, Tom, *Joe Stanley Printer to the Rising* (Dingle, 2005)

Robbins, Frank, *Under the Starry Plough: Recollections of the Irish Citizen Army* (Dublin, 1977)

Robinson, Sir Henry, *Memories: Wise and Otherwise* (London, 1923)

Ross, Sir John, *The Years of my Pilgrimage – Random Reminiscences* (London, 1914)

Royal Commission into the circumstances connected with the Landing of Arms at Howth on July 26th – Report of Commission; and Minutes of Evidence, with appendices and index, 1914

Royal Commission on the Rebellion in Ireland – Report of Commission, 1916.

Royal Commission on the Rebellion in Ireland – Minutes of Evidence and Appendix of Documents, 1916

Royal Commission on the Arrest and Subsequent Treatment of Mr Francis Sheehy-Skeffington, Mr Thomas Dickson, and Mr Patrick James McIntyre – Report of Commission, 1916

Ryan, Desmond, *The Rising: The complete story of Easter Week* (Dublin, 1957)

Scully, Séamus, *The Dublin Rover* (Dublin, 1991)

Setchell, J.R.M., *An Easter Parade – A Bridge too Far: The Irish Rising 1916* (Chesterfield, 2004)

Sinn Féin Rebellion Handbook, Weekly Irish Times, Dublin, 1917

Stephens, James, *The Insurrection in Dublin* (Dublin and London, 1916)

Taaffe, Michael, *Those Days are Gone Away* (London, 1959)

Townshend, Charles, *Easter 1916, The Irish Rebellion* (London, 2005)

Trotsky, Leon, *Trotsky's Writings on Britain*, Vol. 3 (London , 1975)

Willoughby, Roger, *A Military History of the University of Dublin and its Officers Training Corps, 1910-1922* (Limerick, 1989)

Wrench, John Evelyn, *Struggle 1914-1920* (London, 1935)

Periodicals:

AFV News, Jan-Apr 2000, Vol. 35, No. 1, Ontario, 2000

An t-Óglách: The Army Journal, Dublin, Vol. IV – 1926

Blackwood's Magazine, Vol. CXCIX January-June 1916, New York

Blackwood's Magazine, Vol. CC July-December 1916, New York

Capuchin Annual, The, Dublin, 1966

Century magazine, Vol. 93, New York, January 1917

Dublin Historical Record XLI No. 4 September 1988, Dublin, 1988

Eye-Opener, The, Dublin, April 22, 1916

Graphic, The, London, Saturday 6 May-26 August, 1916

Great War, The, Part 103, London, 1916

Ireland of the Welcomes, Vol. 1. No. 6, March-April, 1966

Irish Book Lover, The, Vol. VIII Aug & Sept 1916, Nos 1 & 2, London, 1916

Irish Digest, The, Dublin, April 1939

Irish Journal of Medical Science, Vol. 175, No. 2, April, May, June 2006, Dublin, 2006

Manchester Guardian, The, History of the War, Part L, 16 August 1916, Chapters III & IV

Medal Society of Ireland, Journal of the, No. 57, June 2002

Outlook Magazine, The, New York, May-August, 1916, Vol. 113

Record of the Irish Rebellion of 1916, A, Office of 'Irish Life', Dublin, 1916

Science et Vie, Tome X, No. 27, Paris, Juin-Juillet 1916

Times History of the War, The, Vol. III, London, 1916

Souvenir pictorials:

Bombardment of Lowestoft by the Germans, 25 April, 1916, Lowestoft

Dublin and the 'Sinn Féin Rising', Wilson Hartnell & Co, Dublin, 1916

Dublin and the 'Sinn Féin Rising', Irish Collegiate Club, New York, 1916

Old Ireland in Pictures - including 1916 & 1922, Two Dublin 'Risings' and their Consequences, Wilson Hartnell & Co, Dublin, 1916

Rebellion in Dublin, The, April 1916, Eason & Son Ltd, Dublin and Belfast, 1916

Sinn Féin Rebellion 1916, The, W&G Baird, Belfast, 1916

Sinn Féin Revolt Illustrated, The, Hely's, Dublin, 1916

Sinn Féin Revolt 1916, Twelve Interesting Views, showing the ruins of Sackville Street and adjoining streets after the Rising, John Shuley & Co, The Irish Color Printers, Dublin, 1916

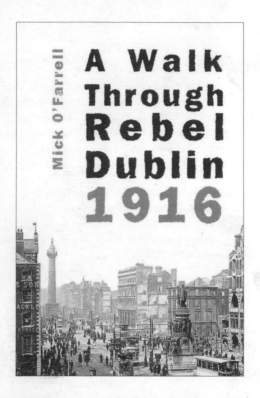

A Walk Through Rebel Dublin 1916

Mick O'Farrell
ISBN: 978 1 85635 276 5

A Walk through Rebel Dublin is a comprehensively illustrated guide
to the Rising of Easter Week 1916, based on significant locations
of the rebellion. Dealing separately with thirty buildings and
sites throughout the city, the author provides a brief, fascinating
history of the events and personalities that dominated these
locations during Easter Week.